Financial Sector Policy and the Poor

Selected Findings and Issues

Patrick Honohan

THE WORLD BANK
Washington, D.C.

printed on recycled paper

1 2 3 4 5 06 05 04

World Bank Working Papers are published to communicate the results of the Bank's work to the development community with the least possible delay. The manuscript of this paper therefore has not been prepared in accordance with the procedures appropriate to formally-edited texts. Some sources cited in this paper may be informal documents that are not readily available.

ISBN: 0-8213-5967-3
ISSN: 1726-5878

Cover Photo: Lazarus and Dives, Moissac (photograph copyright Alison Stones).
Patrick Honohan is Senior Financial Policy Adviser in the Financial Sector Operations and Policy Department at the World Bank.

Library of Congress Cataloging-in-Publication Data has been requested.

Contents

LIST OF FIGURES

Abstract

This paper presents new empirical evidence on how financial sector policy can help the poor. It is often thought that promotion of specialized microfinance institutions is the best or only way forward. However, a strong mainstream financial system is also pro-poor—perhaps even more so: while mainstream financial depth is measurably associated with lower poverty, for microfinance this is not yet so. The roles played by microfinance and mainstream finance in tackling poverty should be regarded as complementary and overlapping rather than as competing alternatives. The essential similarities between the two will become more evident as individual microfinance firms, or associations of firms, grow to the scale needed for sustainability. Policy design that recognizes the need for larger and stronger microfinance institutions poses no threat to the health of mainstream finance. Such a policy would not impose low interest rate ceilings; nevertheless, the goal of protecting the vulnerable from credit market abuses and prejudice should not be neglected in an effective package of policies favorable to the growth of both micro and mainstream finance.

Acknowledgments

The author owes thanks to Thorsten Beck, Jerry Caprio, Carlos Cuevas, Asli Demirgüç-Kunt, Roland Kpodar, Rodney Lester, Millard Long, Sole Martinez Peria, Jonathan Morduch, Anne Ritchie, Bikki Randhawa, Rich Rosenberg, Sergio Schmukler, Lisa Taber, Marilou Uy, and Dimitri Vittas for helpful suggestions. The views expressed are my own and should not be taken as those of the World Bank. phonohan@worldbank.org.

CHAPTER 1

Introduction

A ccess to financial services is a potentially important means of alleviating poverty, especially when combined with other supports for poor households. Yet microfinance has yet to take off in most countries, reaching only a small segment of the potential market. The industry remains fragmented with most individual microfinance firms operating well below efficient scale.

Although long neglected by mainstream financial firms, it would be a mistake to think that microfinance requires some special alchemy for its functioning. Doctrinal debates over the optimal organizational form and governance structures and over the optimal design and mix of products to be offered by microfinance firms have tended to obscure the essential banality of microfinance. Indeed, the fact that successful microfinance institutions (MFIs) are so diverse—and that, for all their diversity, none have introduced techniques or structures that are really new to finance—strongly suggests that, at a deep level, there is nothing special about microfinance. Common sense, cost control, and skilled attention to the demands and sensitivities of the local clientele seem to be the main requirements, along with the ambition to achieve scale. (It is the application of these mundane but essential virtues to a poor clientele that constitutes the revolutionary element). Enabling this to be accomplished, whether by non-governmental organization (NGO)-backed entities, cooperatives, or capitalist firms, should be the guiding principle of policy in regard to microfinance.

However, policy also needs to be aware of the likely limitations of microfinance for achieving a rapid reduction in national absolute poverty levels. Careful impact studies offer little hope that microfinance can make the decisive breakthrough in this regard. Instead, a broad-based acceleration of national economic growth is also needed, and this requires an effective mainstream financial system.

Promoting the development of mainstream finance entails no compromise with a focus on poverty. Indeed, the indications are that finance-intensive development is associated with lower poverty at given levels of mean national per capita income. (The link between healthy finance and poverty reduction is likely to be even stronger along the dimension of openness and contestability, though statistical evidence of this has so far proved elusive.)

Conversely, promoting the growth of microfinance need not threaten mainstream finance. Scale is an issue here from several points of view. In financial terms, mainstream finance is vastly larger than microfinance, whether measured in terms of asset stocks or flows. Thus even a healthy microfinance sector will not divert or absorb lendable funds on a scale that is significant for mainstream finance. Furthermore, the risks of failure of microfinance institutions need to be kept in this perspective of comparative scale. Financial crashes in mainstream finance across the world have caused—and continue to have the potential to cause—poverty-deepening fiscal and overall economic costs far in excess of anything likely to be associated with the failure of microfinance firms.

Protecting the vulnerable from exploitative abuse of debt contracts by the unscrupulous is a goal that deserves greater attention than it has hitherto been accorded in financial sector policy for developing countries. Likewise, attention should also be focused on the possible neglect of ethnic or regional groups in financial sector development. These are not easy problems to resolve, especially in low income countries. Yet, ignoring them leaves the door open to the risk of populist adoption of false remedies such as binding interest rate (usury) ceilings and other forms of intrusive regulation that hamper the healthy functioning of mainstream and microfinance. Nevertheless, design of corrective policies against predatory lending, redlining, and similar issues is in its infancy. Lessons from the United States and other advanced economies which have tried to tackle these issues may currently offer more in the nature of guiding principles than of practical tools that are adapted well to the institutional environment of the developing economies.

Though much of the discussion focuses on the credit side, largely because both available data and the prior literature concentrates there, it should be evident that noncredit financial services including savings and money transmission are also of crucial importance.

The paper is organized as follows. Chapter 2 provides an initial quantification, documenting the wide variation in penetration rates (and reporting on econometric attempts— spelled out in Appendix A—to explain these variations) and the fact that microfinance is uniformly much smaller than the mainstream in terms of assets.

Chapter 3 discusses the degree to which, and the dimensions along which, microfinance should be considered as different from mainstream finance and asks what is stopping microfinance from reaching its full potential, relative to the mainstream. This chapter reports new econometric evidence (spelled out in Appendix B) on the importance on economies of scale at the institutional level.

Chapter 4 reviews the literature on impact, stressing the need to moderate the overoptimistic expectations for microfinance of some non-specialists. In contrast, mainstream finance is shown in cross-country analysis to have a strong pro-poor dimension: its development helps lower national poverty rates (microfinance penetration, by contrast, does not seem to be robustly associated with poverty rates; new econometric evidence on these points is spelled out in Appendix C).

Chapter 5 offers some remarks on alternatives to usury laws and to special public institutions as potential approaches to the need to protect the vulnerable from predatory lending and prejudice. Concluding remarks are in Chapter 6.

CHAPTER 2

Microfinance Penetration

Non-uniform Development of Microfinance Across Countries

Direct access by the poor to financial services is only one aspect of the interaction between finance and poverty, but it is one that has received considerable attention in recent years with the rise of interest in microfinance. Of course, it is important to bear in mind that not all of microfinance involves direct access by the poor to financial services. The term is indeed a rather elastic one, and is often used to include a wider clientele of the near poor and even of microenterprises controlled by entrepreneurs who are not poor.

Few developing countries are now without a sizable number of MFIs, and on some measures there are tens of thousands of MFIs worldwide. Yet, the development of microfinance over the past couple of decades has not been a uniform process, but has been concentrated in a small set of countries. As will now be shown, this is evident from available data, regardless of whether that is expressed as a percentage of population served (or of the poor population), or in terms of total assets, compared with the rest of the financial system or with Gross Domestic Product (GDP).

It has to be said that defining penetration data on a comparable basis in this area is not straightforward, partly because organizational forms and other institutional arrangements differ from country to country with the result that the inclusiveness of national concepts of microfinance varies. In addition, there are several areas of ambiguity or uncertainty about how the boundary defining microfinance should be defined. Small-scale finance provided by mainstream financial institutions is one area of doubt: should this be included or not? Another point on which the literature is not unanimous is whether semi-formal cooperative savings and credit associations should be included. Also, especially on the savings side, many larger intermediaries, including postal savings banks and agricultural development banks—as well as mainstream banks, provide some financial services (mainly deposits) at the micro level even though they are not specialized in microfinance.

In using what is available to obtain a general overall indication of penetration of microfinance, measures based on population are arguably more robust than those based on total assets, because the highly-skewed distribution of total assets means that a small change in the inclusiveness of a measure (to include somewhat larger borrowers) will have a much larger impact on total assets than on numbers of customers.

One source, covering 55 developing countries, is the report from the Microcredit Summit (Daley-Harris 2003). This source focuses on access to credit and on specialized microfinance institutions (though it does include many credit unions and development banks, for example). These are important restrictions.

Christen and others (2004) is a new alternative inventory of penetration data compiled at the Consultative Group to Assist the Poor (CGAP) which spreads a wider net by including both deposit and loan accounts and also going beyond the usual purview of microfinance by sweeping in a range of additional "alternative financial institutions."[1] The total number of accounts in this wider net is "well over 750 million." The Christen data suggests that specialized microfinance firms account for less than one-fifth of the total of such client accounts, with postal savings banks alone accounting for one-half and agricultural development banks and other development banks adding most of the remainder—notably in China and India.[2]

Returning to the Microcredit Summit data, it is clear that, even at the level of the individual institution, the size distribution across the world is highly skewed. (This is not the same as saying that the industry is concentrated, because each reporting institution is confined to a single country). Between them, the 30 largest MFIs account for more than 90 per cent of the clients served worldwide by the 234 top firms (and hence for more than three-quarters of those served by all of the 2572 firms reporting to the Microcredit Summit).

Aggregating up to the national level, the skewed pattern continues to be evident. Table 1 shows that in just eight countries has microfinance broken through an apparent ceiling of 2 per cent of total population. There is a long tail of developing countries—35 of the 55 reporting developing countries—in which MFIs claim fewer than 1 per cent of the population as clients (Figure 1a). The

Table 1a: MFI Penetration Rates—Top Countries (borrowing clients as % of population)			
Bangladesh	13.1	Senegal	1.6
Indonesia	6.7	Nepal	1.5
Thailand	6.5	Mali	1.5
Sri Lanka	4.3	Niger	1.4
Vietnam	4.3	Honduras	1.2
Cambodia	3.0	El Salvador	1.2
Malawi	2.6	Nicaragua	1.1
Togo	2.4	India	1.1
Gambia, The	1.7	Bolivia	1.1
Benin	1.7	Ethiopia	0.9

Source: Based on Daley-Harris (2003).

1. I am greatly indebted to Rich Rosenberg and his co-authors at CGAP for making their data available pre-publication, allowing the analysis of the present paper to take account of this important new source.

2. The cross-country correlation between penetration rates calculated from the Microcredit Summit and credit penetration rates calculated from the Christen and others (2004) data is quite high at 0.7. Further discussion of these data sources is in Appendix A.

Table 1b:	*Borrowing Clients at "Alternative Financial Institutions"*—Top Countries (borrowing clients as % of population)		
Sri Lanka	17.9	Honduras	4.2
Indonesia	13.6	Bulgaria	4.2
Bangladesh	12.7	Ecuador	3.9
Vietnam	8.1	China	3.6
Guatemala	7.8	Benin	3.6
Bolivia	5.9	Gambia	3.6
Egypt	5.8	Nepal	3.6
Cambodia	4.6	Mali	3.6
Myanmar	4.3	Thailand	3.5
Nicaragua	4.2	Uruguay	3.2

Source: Based on Christen and others (2004).

same pattern emerges whether we normalize by total population or by the poor population (Figure 2, which uses the $2 a day measure).

Thus there is a remarkable variation in the degree to which the potential market for micro-credit is being served in different countries.[3] A handful of countries stand out from the rest, especially Bangladesh, Indonesia, Thailand, and Sri Lanka, with Vietnam and Bolivia also indicating high penetration on most definitions.

In effect, there appears to be a *threshold effect* for national penetration of MFIs. Relatively few countries have reached an MFI penetration rate above 1 per cent of population (of course a much higher share of households), or in terms of total loans a sum equivalent to 1 per cent of national M2, but those that have crossed the threshold have broken through to much higher penetration ratios.

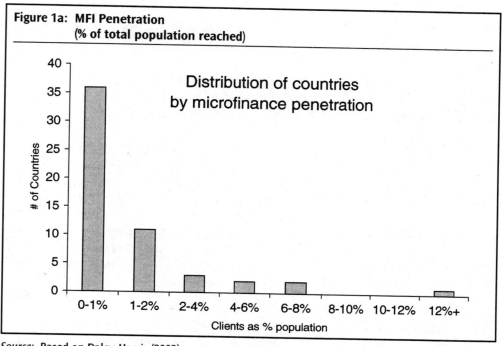

Figure 1a: **MFI Penetration**
(% of total population reached)

Distribution of countries by microfinance penetration

Source: Based on Daley-Harris (2003).

---

3. The coefficient of variation (standard deviation divided by mean) is high at 1.83. (A similar figure is obtained for the wider Christen and others data—1.65 for credit, 1.82 for deposit accounts).

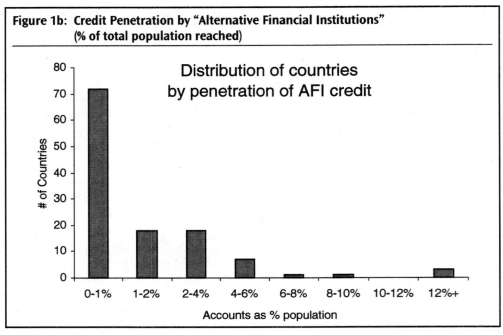

**Figure 1b: Credit Penetration by "Alternative Financial Institutions"
(% of total population reached)**

Distribution of countries
by penetration of AFI credit

Source: Based on Christen et al. (2004).

The more comprehensive data collected at the regional level[4] provides general confirmation of the levels of microfinance penetration and of the wide differences, especially for Latin America (Figure 3).

Even with the much wider definition of "alternative financial institutions" used by Christen and others (2004), credit penetration is not much better. Just 5 of 119 countries covered in the larger data set have credit penetration of over 6 per cent of population, 12 have over 4 per cent (see Figure 1b).[5]

In an attempt to discover what national characteristics make for deeper microfinance penetration, a regression analysis of the cross-country variation in MFI penetration ratios was carried out on the worldwide data and is reported in Appendix A. Although there is no strong relationship between penetration rates and potential determinants such as poverty headcount (Figure 4), a statistically significant regression has been identified. A large population, a high GNP per capita (or low poverty) and poor institutions may be associated with *lower* penetration of MFIs. The results are consistent with the idea that the presence of a market for microfinance (e.g. many poor people) and good country institutions help the microfinance industry grow.

---

4. There have been several regional cross-country compilations, for example Christen (2001) for Latin America, Charitonenko and others (2002, 2003) on several Asian countries; Forster et al. (2003) for Eastern Europe and Central Asia; Brandsma (2004) on the Middle East and North Africa, on all of which we draw here for comparative data.

5. It is in deposits that the wider set of "alternative financial institutions" make a really substantial difference: a third of the countries included show deposit penetration of over 8 per cent. Note that none of the available datasets deals comprehensively with insurance or payments services.

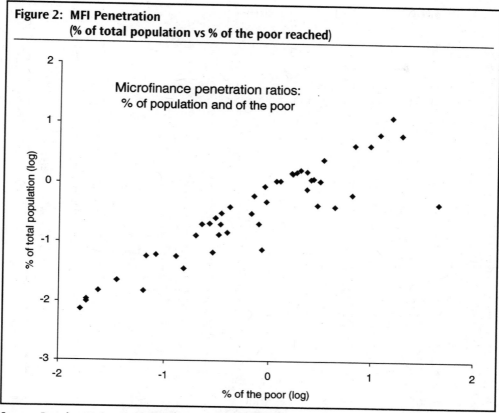

Figure 2: MFI Penetration
(% of total population vs % of the poor reached)

Microfinance penetration ratios:
% of population and of the poor

Source: Based on Daley-Harris (2003); World Bank Global Poverty and Inequality Database.

There is also the suggestion (further discussed below) from these findings that excess profitability of mainstream intermediation can discourage microfinance enterprise. However, most of the cross country variation is not explained by available variables. Other, unmeasured, factors must be important, likely including enforced usury laws and other microfinance-specific pre-conditions. The factors for which data are available can do little to explain what it is that allows a country's microfinance industry to jump the threshold into high penetration. It may be that microfinance penetration takes time; certainly several of the leading countries are also those who have been conspicuously in the business for a long time. However, observation in the present context of this important empirical fact does no more than slightly shift the focus of the question.

Microfinance is Too Small to Threaten the Mainstream

The total assets of microfinance institutions are very small relative to mainstream finance—even in countries which have reached high levels of penetration and are considered by specialists as being close to saturation for microfinance. This is shown in Figure 5 which, although it presents data on only a limited set of countries, does include most of the

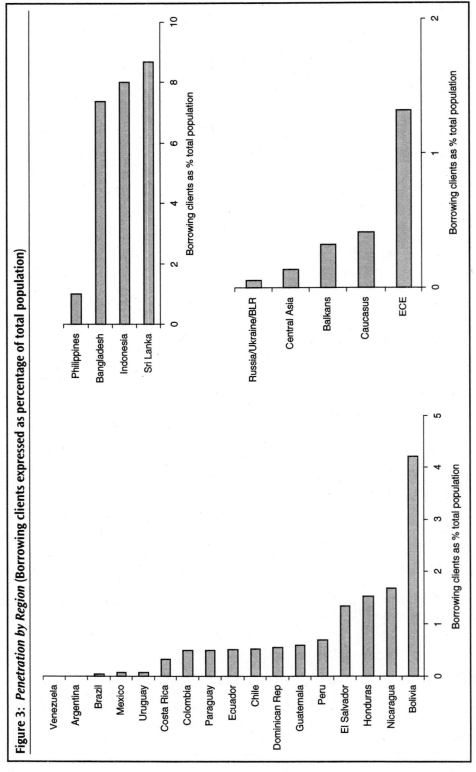

Figure 3: *Penetration by Region* (Borrowing clients expressed as percentage of total population)

Source: Christen (2001), Forster et al. (2003), Charitonenko et al. (2002, 2003); *World Development Indicators.*

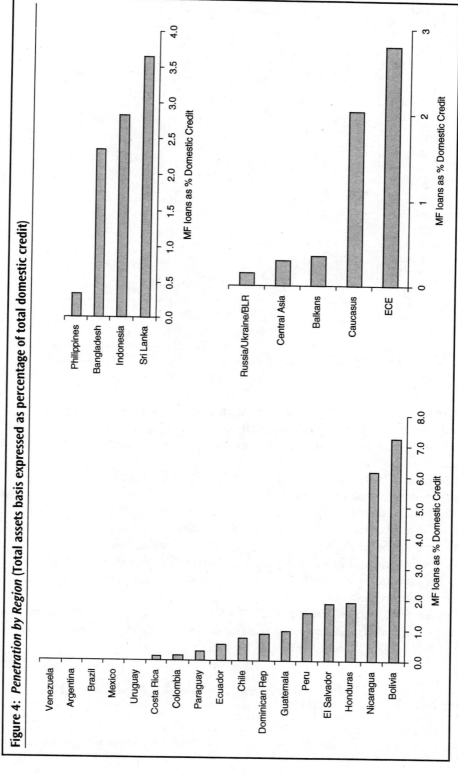

Figure 4: *Penetration by Region* (Total assets basis expressed as percentage of total domestic credit)

Source: Christen (2001), Forster (2003), Charitonenko (2002, 2003); *International Financial Statistics.*

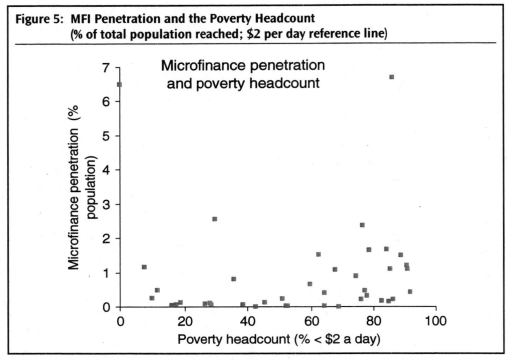

Figure 5: MFI Penetration and the Poverty Headcount
(% of total population reached; $2 per day reference line)

Source: Based on Daley-Harris (2003); World Bank Global Poverty and Inequality Database.

countries which have achieved a relatively high penetration of microfinance.[6] Neverthe-less, and even though most of these countries do not have very deep mainstream financial systems, the highest ratio to M2 achieved by microfinance is about 7 per cent. For most countries the ratio is a lot lower.

It follows that the direct risks to systemic financial stability from insolvency of microfinance institutions must be limited by their small scale. Yes, to the extent that such institutions take deposits from low income households, the consequences for these households could be severe; small firms could also be affected with localized knock-problems. Yet, the scale of the insolvency could rarely be large in relation to GDP or to mainstream finance simply because the total assets (and *a fortiori* the total domestic liabilities) of micro-finance intermediaries are small. The potential threat to mainstream finance from micro-finance insolvency is small.

Furthermore, even where penetration of its target market is high, microfinance absorbs only a small fraction of available loanable funds. In effect it does not compete with conventional finance for such funds.

_____

6. Figures 4 and 5 show data from three different regional studies: Christen (2001) for Latin America; Forster and others (2003) for Central and Eastern Europe and Central Asia; four studies by Charitonenko with co-authors (2002, 2003) for different Asian countries. The data refers to borrowing clients and loans. Although not using comparable inclusion criteria across regions (for example, the ECA study includes credit unions, whereas these are excluded from the LAC study), it is noteworthy that the main features of this data set—small and highly variable penetration rates—echo those of the Microcredit Summit data used above.

CHAPTER 3

Is Microfinance Different to the Mainstream?

The contrasts between microfinance and the mainstream are frequently overdrawn by observers. Although casual observation of the way in which the typical microfinance entity operates reveals some striking differences by comparison with the typical mainstream bank, it is arguable that these differences are superficial. The extensive commonalities shared by the two forms of finance are more important in assessing the future of microfinance than are the differences.

Differences Related to Scale, Style, and Subsidy

Three major dimensions along which microfinance can appear to be different are *scale*, *style* of operation, and *subsidy*. In each case, the appearance of difference needs to be qualified. Yes, most MFIs are small by comparison with the typical bank, but this can be seen as a transitional phenomenon. Indeed, as we show below, sustainability of an MFI is partly a function of scale. Subsidy certainly exists now, but should be not seen (and is not seen by many microfinance enthusiasts) as essential to the health and sustainability of an microfinance industry. The essential features of the financial relationships employed by MFIs are by no means novel in the history of finance, formal and informal. (This is not to deny that there is a new wave of application of these techniques to deliver unsecured credit to poor clients in poor countries.)

Although evolving technology continues to change the calculations in this regard, microfinance has entailed high labor costs per dollar of transactions. Creation and strategic management of a large labor-intensive enterprise of this type calls for abilities that are not widely distributed. To the extent that a sheltered, profitable mainstream financial sector offers a better rate of return to such entrepreneurial and managerial skills, the micro-finance sector will continue to lack this key factor. Of course, few mainstream bankers are ready and able to switch into the microfinance business in response to changing incentives, but there can be an effect at the margin. Regulatory policy should be designed to ensure that entry into microfinance remains easy, and that the mainstream sector is not over-protected and unduly profitable.

Scale

The fact that just a few countries have managed to achieve penetration ratios that break through the 1 per cent threshold has already been noted. Those that have made the breakthrough display no unique pattern of organizational form, product mix, degree of subsidization, etc. One thing these countries *do* have in common is that their micro-finance industry is concentrated and dominated by large-scale operations. In countries such as Bangladesh, Indonesia and Sri Lanka, which have made that breakthrough, just a handful of institutions are carrying the bulk of the business, both in dollar terms and number of clients (with the five-firm concentration ratio amounting to at least 75 per cent in these countries). Achieving scale of individual institutions, rather than having a large number of MFIs, seems to be the key to ensuring that the sector has reached a large proportion of the population.[7] This point would be reinforced if we were to add in the additional alternative financial institutions—most of them large—counted by Christen and others (2004).

Market structure as well as the need to spread fixed costs could be relevant here. The incentive for borrowers to repay can be eroded by the presence of multiple alternative lenders. While this problem arises with even a few lenders, it can be managed through information sharing as long as the market is not too fragmented. A social optimum would, however, preserve a degree of competition, while strengthening information infrastructures.

Among MFIs, size is positively associated with financial viability. This is known from a variety of micro studies, though these tend to indicate that economies of scale peter out beyond a certain point. Further evidence of scale economies is shown in Appendix B, which reports new regression findings based on data in the *Microbanking Bulletin*'s published data-base. A doubling of scale is associated with an increase in the self-sufficiency index (operating income as a percentage of expenses) of between 6 and 10 percentage points and the effect is statistically significant. The size of individual loans also seems to matter, whether these are measured by average loan size or by the fraction of loans of less than US$300 made by the institution: bigger loans mean more self-sufficiency.[8] (Curiously, if loan size is normalized by national per capita income, the effect is reversed; this seems to be attributable to a country factor rather than an institutional one).

---

7. Note that it is not just that big institutions are found in countries with extensive coverage, but that in countries with extensive coverage the industry is concentrated: we find no countries where extensive coverage has been achieved by a myriad of small institutions.

8. The poorer the client and the smaller the size of individual loans or other transactions, the less chance that these services can be delivered at any realistic price. For this and other reasons, some authors are skeptical about the ability of MFIs to provide credit on a commercial basis to very poor clients. Nevertheless, the ability of informal moneylenders to reach a very poor clientele should not be forgotten in this context.

These correlations could have many interpretations. It is not clear that we are simply estimating a cost function. For example, cost-control resulting in financial viability removes the funding barrier to institutional expansion. Again, it may be that those MFIs that have chosen to focus on small loans (to the poor) are doing so as part of a grant-aided mandate; if so, absorbing the grant funding will result in accounts that show such MFIs to be financially non-viable.

The importance of achieving scale is also underlined by the consideration that, when economic shocks that can plunge households into poverty are regionwide, then (as with informal finance) small-scale and geographically confined financial arrangements are unable to dissipate the risk through pooling. Though effective against temporary and idiosyncratic risks, the ability of the financial network in which poor households participate to insulate these households from shocks that have wider and more longer-lasting impacts depends on its interconnectedness with the national (and even global) finance.[9]

Subsidy

Perhaps no aspect of microfinance has been the subject of more discussion than the degree of subsidy which it has typically entailed. A large fraction of these institutions benefit from subsidy, whether in the form of technical assistance, an endowment of capital not expected to be remunerated, or a flow of funds for onlending provided at below market rates. Overall, the MFI sector remains heavily grant and subsidy dependent. Although the percentage fell during the late 1990s, by end-2000 the largest market, that of Bangladesh, still relied on grants and soft loans for 41% of its rapidly-growing revolving loan fund (Charitonenko and Rahman 2002).[10] Lending rates have been increasing, as has the incidence and scale of lump sum charges, yet most MFIs are still not operating on a self-sufficient basis.[11]

A case in point is that of the second largest microcredit provider in the developing world, Grameen Bank, which still relies on subsidies.[12] Some have seized on this to criticize other elements of Grameen's functioning (the regimentation and the limited range of

---

9. How is the experience of the Unit Desa system of Indonesia's BRI to be interpreted in this light? As is well-known, loan recovery performance of this entity continued to be strong through Indonesia's severe macroeconomic and financial crisis of 1997–98. It seems that this shock emerged in the formal, urban sector and had a relatively smaller impact on the rural areas where BRI Unit Desa was most active. Rapid inflation will also have eroded the real value of loans and made repayment more affordable. Though connected with the wider Indonesian financial system, BRI Unit Desa was not contractually vulnerable to a withdrawal of funding from the rest of the system (Patten and others 2001).

10. Even the World Bank contributes in a substantial way to these subsidies. The $150 million IDA credit approved in 2001 to finance below-market onlending to MFIs by the Bangladeshi apex PSKF is a case in point. The sum involved may be compared with total MFI loans outstanding in Bangladesh at end-2000 of less than $700 million.

11. In Bangladesh, a 15 percent "flat rate" (i.e. charged on the initial loan throughout the period of loan without regard to amortization payments) was reported in 2002 as the typical rate, and is the ceiling rate for loans financed from the apex PSKF. Rates have been rising, and some MFI lenders charge 20 percent flat. In recent years, bank lending rates in Bangladesh reported as IFS line 60p have edged up from 14 to 16 percent (declining balance rates).

12. A high fraction of Grameen's below-cost funding is invested in money market instruments rather than lent to clients: the net interest helps to pay administrative expenses. Several other large MFIs, including BRI, also maintain very high money market investments.

financial services offered) as being incompatible with financial sustainability. Yet, it is clear that the main reason for Grameen's lack of financial sustainability is its decision not to charge a high enough interest rate (Grameen's rates are lower than those of self-financing MFIs.) If there were no subsidy, Grameen would have to charge more, and would surely do so. The demand for their credit is not likely to fall off drastically at the moderately higher levels of interest needed. Despite the higher loan losses experienced in recent years, a high-interest Grameen would surely be potentially sustainable; the current slight-loss-making strategy is a management choice.

Further, it is a widely-held aspiration among many of the donors to MFIs that they should become self-sufficient and as such sustainable in the medium-term.[13] Cost efficiency and convenience are hallmarks of sustainable operations.[14]

Of course the problems of rent-seeking and roundtripping associated with subsidized loan funds are well recognized in the literature. There can be little justification now for donor or government programs that provide funds for on-lending at below-market interest rates (though there are still many such programs!). Where there is room for debate is the role of: (i) subsidies designed as a way of overcoming set-up costs;[15] and (ii) subsidized educational and other ancillary programs operated in conjunction with microfinance.

Subsidy for microfinance of either of these more refined types is sometimes seen in too negative a light, as if the fiscal or donor resources used are necessarily being wasted. This need not be so. The effectiveness of such uses of public money (the subsidy element), must be considered primarily on their own merits as grant-aid targeted at poverty reduction. Even if effectively targeted to the very poor (which is questionable), does subsidized microcredit really represent the most effective use of the scarce public funds available for grant-aiding anti-poverty measures? Probably not—though there are likely to be less effective uses, too.

Effectively targeted anti-poverty microfinance subsidies are unlikely to damage mainstream finance. Specific cases of assistance to the extremely poor in which microcredit is bundled with food-aid or education[16] can hardly damage the functioning of the commercial financial system even if sustained over a long period, given that such destitute beneficiaries would never have had access to a commercial financial intermediary[17] and that the total volume of such loans is negligible in the context of the financial system as a whole. The distorting side-effects on the functioning of the micro-finance entity through which the subsidy flows is likely to be greater than any effect on the wider financial system. However,

---

13. The potential effect of commercialization in reducing the extent to which MFIs reach the poorest is an important topic not considered here (Christen 2001).

14. Frontier performance in this regard may be defined by BRI of Indonesia, whose village units achieve a productivity of 1300 clients per employee (though note that 85 percent of these clients are savers). Yet customers may have to travel up to 30km to the nearest (one-room) branch of BRI. (Some other MFIs use mobile units and lockboxes to bring partial or intermittent savings services closer to the client).

15. In addition to many of the subsidies provided by donors to the MFIs that they sponsor, this would be the case of the Chilean program which auctioned a small per loan subsidy for microloans made by licensed intermediaries.

16. As with the IGVGD program in Bangladesh giving a household with income of less than $6 per month a sack of grain as well as a loan sufficient to buy a few dozen chickens. (The flow of eggs laid and sold can more than cover the interest cost; Hashemi and Tudor 2003, Matin and Hulme 2003).

17. In the example provided, ability to service the microloan is dependent on receiving the sack of grain.

when subsidized funds for onlending are available and channeled to microborrowers on a large scale, this will surely discourage the emergence of unsubsidized microfinance entities.[18]

To be sure, at present, funding for MFIs is not widely seen as the key constraint. Indeed, there is an apparent paradox in juxtaposing two well-accepted propositions in microfinance. On the one hand, a mantra of microfinance specialists is that the main constraint on the healthy expansion of the sector is not a flow of investible funds, but a network of robust retail delivery outlets.[19] On the other hand, the vision of microfinance enthusiasts is graduation of MFIs from reliance on donor funds on the ground that the flow of these funds will prove insufficient and unreliable. The paradox can be resolved by clarifying the time-frame and scale of operations which the two propositions are considering. The first looks to the immediate prospects and the great current enthusiasm of donors for expanding microfinance from a base which is, in most countries, low in relation to perceived needs or demand. The second looks to a longer term, and to a microfinance industry vastly larger than the present one, in which case an ability to self-finance would prove essential.[20]

Style

In considering the differences in style of operation between microfinance and the mainstream, it is important to realize the diversity within microfinance itself. Diversity and experimentation has been the hallmark of the recent development of microfinance. Microfinance institutions as a group defy simple summary descriptions that would do justice to their variety even within individual countries, and even more so across countries.[21, 22]

It is in their lending technology that microfinance firms have often seemed different to the mainstream. The practice of group lending in particular has received great emphasis from theoreticians seeking to understand how modern microfinance deals with information, enforcement and administrative costs. The literature focuses on the potential for

---

18. Nor can the funds be expected to trickle-down reliably. The monopolistic competition models of Hoff and Stiglitz (1997) illustrate the havoc which additional availability of subsidized funds can create in the informal credit market by encouraging entry, with the result that more lenders are paying set-up costs (potentially resulting in *higher* onlending rates), and enforcement may be more costly as borrowers have more alternative options for future borrowing.

19. Sometimes delivering more than financial services (see Dunford 2003)—though this is controversial and many scholars think that MFIs should stick to financial services.

20. As the sector expands, the marginal social value of further expansion would decline, and donors would naturally and rationally begin to switch funding to areas of greater need.

21. Even the definition of microfinance is rather elastic. In the use of all writers, the term includes all financial services provided directly to the poor, however defined, but in addition lending to near-poor households, self-employed individuals and microenterprises whether defined in terms of a ceiling on turnover, assets or employment—for example, 3 to 5 to 10 employees—are also covered. In practice, much more arbitrary cut-offs, such as maximum loan size (for example, maximum loan of $3,000–$5,000) are used. This looseness of terminology reflects not only availability of data, but also contrasting local economic structures as well as the policy focus of the author in question.

22. An additional dimension is in the type of target group chosen by the MFI. Some focus on women, some on poor clients, some on small business lending, etc. For NGOs this is not merely a business decision: helping the target group improve their economic performance or social and psychological wellbeing is often the main goal of the promoting organization. Measuring the degree to which the target group has indeed been reached can thus be, in itself, a significant task for such NGOs, especially since determining the degree of poverty of a client is not methodologically unproblematic.

implicit side-contracts among group members who have lower costs of information with regard to their fellow-members, and on the effectiveness for enforcement of social sanctions between group members. Even without such information, advantages can be gained from group lending (Ghatak and Guinnane 1999).[23] Other features highlighted by observers have been the progressive increase in the amount lent to an individual or group members as each successive loan is repaid, the use of non-traditional collaterals (notably those that likely to be of more value to the borrower than the lender) and high frequency of required repayment instalments. All of these represent relatively obvious techniques to cope with information problems such as moral hazard (progressive lending enhances the incentive to repay early loans; the discipline effect of collateral depends not on its resale value, but on its value to the debtor; high frequency of payments reduces the free-cash problem).

Early imitators of the Grameen Bank model originally tended to adopt with at most minor amendments a very specific form of group lending technology employing small groups with a specific staggered progressive lending schedule (with borrowers' access to further credit dependent on repayment by the other group members), an element of forced saving and a ritual of regular group meetings. Yet, the accumulation of experience has shown that an increasingly wide range of lending products can be successfully employed. There is a clear trend in microfinance entities worldwide toward increased flexibility of products. Larger groups, different maturities, individual rather than group lending, flexible savings schemes— all of these have become commonplace in microfinance today and seem to work well (Rutherford 2001, Armendáriz de Aghion and Morduch 2004). Higher interest rates are also part of the trend. So far, observers have not reported that these developments have worsened loan-loss experience, though this aspect deserves more study. The original Grameen model, once considered the *sine qua non* of microlending, is increasingly being criticized as unduly rigid, and has been superseded even in Grameen Bank itself. Seemingly a latter-day cargo cult, the Grameen model worked, but perhaps not only or even mainly because of these particularly innovative dimensions of its lending technology.

Business models and product and service technologies of microfinance institutions now arguably differ more widely across countries, and even between different microfinance entities within a given country than does formal finance. This partly reflects the still-experimental nature of much of modern microfinance, as witnessed by the extensive case study literature on NGO-led and other start-up MFIs. (Not all of these experiments work; the many examples of MFI collapse are sometimes glossed-over in discussion of the sector). However, it also reflects the need for microfinance institutions to adapt their behavior to local conditions (terrain, security, communications, temporal and stochastic properties of income flows and spending needs, family and community relationships, customs, and so forth) to a greater extent than do banks in their dealings with salaried or high income individuals and formal sector enterprises.

As its practices become more diverse, it is becoming less easy to characterize the financial technology of microfinance as something really distinctive and new in the history of finance. Group lending; forced saving as a prerequisite for borrowing; frequent payment

---

23. Theoreticians have also been intrigued by the microeconomic theory of informal rotating credit associations ROSCAs: what makes them attractive to participants, what prevents them from collapsing (Anderson and Baland 2002, Anderson and others 2003). Some of the borrowing groups in Bolivia's Bancosol are said to be composed of the members of former ROSCAs.

schedules; all of these are known well even in European financial history from the practice of a range of institutions from pawnbrokers to industrial insurance companies.

Indeed, a reading of the countless "best practice" manuals in circulation for MFIs confirms that at another level there is no *fundamental* difference between the businesses of banks and MFIs.[24] Both seek to make profitable loans by careful choice of borrower; both seek to contain operating costs, employing standardized contracts where appropriate; both set lending interest rates at levels which can ensure profitability; and—at least if we consider the larger and more progressive MFIs—both recognize the synergies between the provision of credit and other financial services. Indeed, MFIs that reach a certain scale usually[25] opt for a banking license, confirming that banking is indeed their business. While much is made of the cultural differences between conventional banking and MFI banking, notably in regard to the required behavior and training of the loan officers and other staff, it is not clear that the difference is any greater than that between the behavior and training of regular branch staff of a commercial bank and the staff of, say, its "private banking" affiliate directed to serving high-wealth individuals.

Diversity also extends to the organizational forms adopted by microfinance firms, which are now not only (i) charitable and other not-for-profit "non-government organizations" all of which make loans but many of which do not take deposits, but also (ii) savings and credit cooperatives or credit unions, and (iii) regional banks, often rural, controlled by local authorities, as well as (iv) for-profit intermediaries specializing, perhaps through an affiliate, in microfinance. The relative importance of these organizational forms in different parts of the world is startlingly different. There appears to be *no dominant organizational form.* The most widespread organizational form (whether NGO, credit cooperative, regional bank, or formal bank) differs from region to region and from country to country—even as between the countries which have achieved high penetration. For example, in Eastern Europe and Central Asia, credit unions predominate overall (though not in the Balkans or in Central Asia), whereas in Bangladesh it is predominantly NGOs;[26] in Indonesia it is a large and profit-oriented, albeit state-owned, bank; in the Philippines, regional banks.

It would be easy to overstate this point, and there is no denying that there are many contrasts between the ways in which the fundamentals are being implemented in MFIs and in mainstream banks. The essential point stands, together with its implication—namely that a generalization of microfinance practice to mainstream banking is undoubtedly feasible.

What Prevents Microfinance from Expanding to Full Potential?

Why have so few countries surpassed the penetration threshold, whether using specialized microfinance institutions or even by mainstream banks reaching down?

---

24. A convenient summary in Robinson (2001), pages 80–83 clearly illustrates the point.
25. Unless inhibited from doing so by incentives built into the regulatory framework such as preferences for NGO status.
26. Grameen Bank, though it has a banking license, still evidently falls into category (i) above, as does BRAC.

It is unlikely to be simply a problem of imperfect technology transfer. For one thing microfinance technology is not especially novel, and to the extent that it is, microfinance itself has by now been around long enough for an understanding of its methods to have percolated rather widely. Given the diversity of organizational form and business practice observed even among successful MFIs, it is unlikely that failure in this regard is attributable to choice of the wrong microeconomic model.

Some argue that microfinance is inherently unprofitable, despite the protestations of MFI specialists and many apparently clearcut examples, most conspicuously BRI in Indonesia.[27] There are cases where government action can be blamed. Heavily subsidized government programs have sometimes undercut the profitability of small-scale lending; prudential restrictions on loan contracts (for example, requiring the bank to obtain full collateral for any loan), if enforced, can prevent the use of lending technologies often used in microfinance where collateral is not available.

Instead, a plausible interpretation of the facts is that effective microfinance provision for low income households and low-value added microenterprises is intensive in resources that are not plentiful in developing countries. Most likely these resources involve strategic management. Only when management resources are applied on a sufficiently large scale (whether by commercial bankers, NGO activists, or public servants) will microfinance provision break through the threshold and become firmly established on the scale that has been achieved, for example, in Bangladesh.

The problem is that microfinance is not generally considered very profitable, even when carried out on a large scale. Of course this is debated territory, and there is increasing evidence of relatively high rates of return to capital invested, though not necessarily to entrepreneurship. Yet, the argument does not necessarily depend on this, but only on the perception of limited profit prospects—to which one might add a range of other social barriers to the acceptability among conventional bankers of microfinance. For these or other reasons, microfinance does not attract many persons with the necessary entrepreneurial and strategic management skills. That is why promoters of microfinance for the past two centuries have frequently come from a charitable background rather than entering the industry as an income-enhancing choice. Where entrepreneurs have been present, and where the operation has been planned on a sufficiently large scale, then success has followed in terms of outreach and adequate financial performance. However, the heavy commitment of management time involved in setting up a microfinance program, combined with the modest expected financial returns, means that the establishment of a microfinance program still seems an unattractive proposition to most larger commercial banks—falling below their threshold of interest, especially where banking is highly profitable. Lack of competition in the conventional banking system can contribute to this by raising the return on other uses of management time.

Some evidence in support of this picture is provided in Appendix A which shows that microfinance penetration is negatively associated in cross-country regressions with measures of mainstream bank profitability. If mainstream banking is profitable enough, why

---

27. Whose village banking "unit desa" program has consistently reported profitability despite an absence of subsidies for most of its twenty year life.

would a banker commit scarce entrepreneurial and strategic management skills to the less promising area of microfinance, especially if success in this venture requires operations on quite a large scale?[28]

The policy lessons from this perspective are unproblematic for mainline financial sector policy. As well as being good for the economy, increasing the contestability of finance, thereby removing excess profitability, will tend to make microfinance look relatively more attractive for financial institutions and financial professionals. These will then be more likely to apply themselves to this sector on a sufficient scale complementing the efforts of the cooperative sector. Aiming for scale at the level of the individual institution, while keeping the door open to enterprise in the form of new starts should be the hallmark of the regulatory and licensing approach.

This absolute shortage of entrepreneurial and managerial effort may be overcome gradually. Encouraged by changing technology and increased competition for low-risk clients, and despite having to compete with subsidized institutions, many for-profit banks have begun to explore microfinance. Where these are successful, the banks likely will stay in the market for the long haul (the setup costs having been sunk). Demonstration effects will attract others.

What then is the future for the many smaller NGOs, credit cooperatives/credit unions, and rural banks which now populate the microfinance segment? Many of these are poorly managed, heavily reliant on subsidy, and vulnerable to waves of loan delinquency and even fraud. They scarcely belong to the world of modern finance, failing to exploit economies of scale or diversification. Many, but not all. Some represent a pool of experimentation yielding significant externalities.[29] Some (especially the cooperatives/credit unions and perhaps some rural banks) are structured so as to exploit social capital in a way that will continue to be of value especially if they can rely on umbrella organizations to help overcome scale and diversification shortcomings.

There is thus the prospect that, one by one, individual countries will see the management of a handful of institutions make the leap into provision of microfinance on a relatively large scale. In doing so they almost surely will rely on a bankable model that in no *fundamental* way differs from textbook practice, even though, culturally and in almost every *superficial* detail, microfinance and the mainstream are at present poles apart.

Policy Implications

If, as is here being suggested, success in surpassing the threshold requires scarce strategic management resources that are more highly rewarded elsewhere in the economy (including in oligopolized conventional financial sectors), the policy conclusion is that entry should

---

28. Of course this neglects the role, highly important up to now, of NGO promoters and providers of microfinance services. See Rutherford (2000) on the distinction between promoters and providers and the difficulties encountered by many promoters in making their innovations organizationally self-sustaining.

29. An example would be Safe-save of Dhaka: with just 7,000 clients probably still too small in its scale, and (like many of the most innovative NGOs) surely dependent on strategic management that has a high but unmeasured opportunity cost. Yet, the techniques it is piloting are considered pathbreaking in microfinance, and the experiment is of wide value.

be encouraged (to facilitate the entry of all-too-scarce entrepreneurs), but smallness of scale dynamically discouraged.[30] Competitiveness of the mainstream sector should be enhanced. Microfinance employs traditional financial tools, but clearly calls for significant adaptations by commercial banks hoping to participate.

More generally, the emergent consensus on what should be regarded as "best practice" for the development of the microfinance sector, though designed with the focus clearly on that sector, turns out to be wholly concordant with the emergence of stronger and more effective mainstream finance.[31, 32] This is largely because commercialization and professionalization of the sector is the goal of microfinance advocates and the supporting donors. Thus, progressive avoidance of heavy reliance on subsidies, and increased use of modern credit appraisal techniques, including credit information systems (though these will never fully replace personal underwriting), are seen as goals for microfinance just as they are also required conditions for the improved functioning of the commercial financial sector. The improvements in legal and information infrastructure that are required to enhance the performance of microfinance also help the performance of the rest of the financial system. An example, currently relevant in Bangladesh—the world center of microfinance—would be making provision for the establishment of a security interest in movable property (Charitonenko and Rahman 2002).

The key policy questions that may impact the development of the commercial financial system here relate to deposit-taking licenses and the intensity of regulation. First, deposit-taking MFIs could collapse, adversely affecting the commercial system; second, the prudential regulation of deposit-taking MFIs could prove to be an administrative burden that distracts supervisors from doing an adequate job in protecting the safety-and-soundness of the main system. The Consensus Guidelines on MFI regulation (Christen and others 2003) take a balanced view on these matters, arguing that deposit-taking on a small scale may be allowed essentially to go unsupervised (especially in cases where the deposits only come in the form of forced-savings components of the lending product, so that most depositors are net borrowers from the MFI at most times). This approach leaves the supervisory appara-

---

30. This phrase is meant to convey the idea of a regulatory approach that, while it permits the establishment of small MFIs, is scrutinized to ensure that it minimizes threshold effects in regulations acting as barriers to the expansion of individual institutions (for example, imposing reporting requirements only on institutions that reach a certain size—note that such threshold effects cannot always be easily avoided, as in the case mentioned below of small deposit taking institutions), that facilitates mergers between well-performing MFIs and that offers inducements to scale such as easing access to the payments system by larger MFIs.

31. These remarks refer to those policy aspects that have a bearing on the wider financial sector. Much of this "best practice" program has no such bearing, being specific to MFI management (as with improving management information and achieving cost efficiencies) and program design (as with efforts to overcome cultural resistence).

32. This is true even of relaxations, urged by microfinance proponents, of what are in fact unduly restrictive rules limiting the scale of uncollateralized loans and on the level of documentation required for small loans; these can constrain wholesaling of loans through MFIs by licensed intermediaries. Ownership restrictions on MFIs (designed to limit concentrations of wealth) can also be usefully relaxed in the case of the licensing small or verifiably socially-oriented MFIs.

tus unencumbered by having to deal in depth with a profusion of tiny MFIs.[33] While the Guidelines do not resolve all of the current debates on microfinance regulation (including issues surrounding the common bond in credit cooperatives, minimum capital requirements, and line-of-business and ownership restrictions), they clear much of the ground and provide a firm foundation.

In the interim, and perhaps for the foreseeable future, one expects to see a continued patchwork of MFIs including small local NGO-financed entities lurching from crisis to crisis and dependent on the energy and vision of a few key individuals; larger-scale and more professionally run concerns with tens of thousands of customers also largely employing donor funds but beginning to tap local savings; traditional savings and credit cooperatives relying for central services on a nationwide league;[34] commercial entities with a microfinance window or arm. It is hard to prevent donors from establishing new MFIs even though many prove nonviable and fail or become moribund in a short period. To the extent that this can still be seen as a period of institutional experimentation, and one in which extensive geographical areas are not yet reached either by MFIs or commercial intermediaries, it would be unwise to adopt too negative an approach to this proliferation. In the longer term, however, one can envisage consolidation of the sector to a relatively small number of large—probably nationwide[35]—entities (perhaps along with a more tightly integrated network of credit cooperatives), most of whom will be deposit-taking and subject to prudential regulation.[36] These increasingly will be competing at the margin with commercial intermediaries with credit information being shared (if necessary on a compulsory basis) between commercial and non-commercial entities. This vision is largely unproblematic for either the enthusiasts of microfinance[37] or the guardians of the formal, commercial system. If and when it approaches this vision, microfinance should not present a problem in terms of compromising the sound development of the rest of the financial sector.[38]

---

33. The Consensus Guidelines do not define how the cut-off is to be determined. One can imagine thresholds on the size of individual loans, on the total portfolio size, or on the number of customers. The common bond (community, employment, and so forth) has been a traditional approach in delimiting the scope of lightly regulated institutions, though it is of declining usefulness in the rapidly changing and increasingly urban environment of developing countries today. Some minimal registration and reporting requirements would still be imposed on small deposit-takers, but this could be done on a delegated basis where suggested by geography.

34. Where the individual institutions are small, they have tended to form regional or national umbrella associations to provide shared services; in several cases (such as with credit unions in Central and Eastern Europe), a three-tier system involving both regional and national umbrellas has proved effective.

35. While there may continue to be some wholesaling of funds, notably to surviving isolated smaller MFIs, the future does not appear to lie with a sizable expansion of apex institutions (Levy 2002).

36. Though with light reporting requirements, as argued in the Consensus Guidelines.

37. Though attention needs to be paid to the degree to which existing schemes rely on limited competition. If there are many competitors offering finance, the threat of losing access through failure to repay will tend to decline (Hoff and Stiglitz 1997). Solutions to this challenge (whether at the collective level as in improved credit sharing mechanisms and legal enforcement, or at the level of individual contracts) will tend to accelerate the convergence of micro and mainstream finance.

38. There is, however a tension between safe and sound development of smaller MFIs and their provision of the full range of microfinance services including deposit-based products. The latter is needed for them to make their full potential contribution to poverty reduction among their clients. No attempt is made in this note to resolve that tension.

CHAPTER 4

Impact

Microfinance Impact: Alleviation More than Escape

If we were sure that microfinance had a sizable and reliable effect on poverty, the fact that most countries have not crossed the threshold in microfinance development would become a matter of considerable importance for anti-poverty policy. However, despite an extensive literature about the impact of microfinance on many dimensions of poverty, there are several obstacles to arriving at a robust judgment on this matter. It is not appreciated widely outside the specialist econometrics community just how scarce are reliable estimates of the impact of direct access to financial services on income, expenditure, or wealth of poor households. Instead, it may be that the general public has been misled by selective presentation of evidence into believing wrongly that the poverty impact of microfinance is clear, certain, and substantial.

How to Trace the Impact of Microfinance on Poverty

Even if we ignore the deficiencies of a narrowly welfarist perspective (Sen 2000), it is not altogether clear whether simply measuring changes in income, consumption, and wealth will suffice to produce an adequate picture of the effect of microfinance on poverty. For one thing, the channels of effect are multiple and may take some time to evolve.

In terms of classic economic mechanisms, we can think of the direct effects of access to financial services (see Matin and others 2002) as coming through:[39]

---

39. The three pathways presented, although couched here in financial terms, can also be understood to subsume aspects frequently described in sociological or anthropological terms such as coping, empowerment, etc.

(i) The ability of near-poor households, with expected income levels above the poverty line, to insure themselves against a variety of shocks that could bring their consumption levels below the poverty line, whether temporarily or permanently. In addition to directly insulating against income declines, insurance could have the indirect effect of making households sufficiently confident to engage in riskier high yield economic activities, thereby increasing their productivity and mean income. For low income groups, liquid and secure savings media are at least as relevant here as formal insurance products.[40]

(ii) Access to credit, through which a poor household may acquire capital (physical or human) yielding (in combination with pre-existing resources) a rate of return in excess of cost of credit and thereby enhancing income; and

(iii) A reduction in the cost of making small payments locally, nationally, and internationally on a secure basis.[41]

Even if poverty impact is ultimately to be measured in terms of income, access to financial services may start an elaborate process of development whose ultimate effect on income will not be evident for several years. Just to take one example, consider the evidence uncovered by Beegle, Dehejia, and Gatti (2003) from Tanzania micro-survey data that access at the household level to credit acts as a substitute for child labor.[42] Such an effect will evidently have intergenerational effects whose long-term consequences for measured income poverty are likely to be quite different to the immediate impact.

This particular example highlights the multidimensional and intertemporal nature of the anti-poverty effects that can be relevant. More generally, capital formation made possible by access to finance may not yield its full fruit within the timeframe of most impact studies: increments to household or family income of the substitution of additional schooling for child labor in particular will occur only over a period of time. Risk reduction too need not show up in aggregate income data—after all, increased consumption security for every household in a group need not be associated with any change in group mean incomes.[43] Individual empowerment, along dimensions such as enhanced self-esteem and increased status in the community or (especially for women) in the household, are also likely to have slow-burning income impacts, quite apart from the direct utility they may bring.

---

40. The most common formal insurance product provided to poor people is life insurance, because of its known risks, the limited scope for—or possibility of controlling—moral hazard, adverse selection and fraud (for instance the relative ease of verifying the loss event). Health and property insurance are less easy to establish in low-income environments, though weather-based farm insurance is emerging as a viable product through national and international reinsurance. Insuring the unrepaid portion of a loan against death and other specific risks is also a viable business. Reducing unit costs of servicing insurance through group cover is an important element of most successful microinsurance schemes. For a review of emerging practices in the microinsurance industry in developing countries, see Brown and Churchill (2000). For a discussion of the potential for microinsurance, see Morduch (2003).

41. Reducing the cost of small retail payments is an important aspect of direct access to financial services by the poor, and one which is currently receiving attention thanks to improvements in technology, but it will not be discussed further here.

42. This is consistent with cross-country evidence relating child labor or debt bondage to mainstream financial development (Dehejia and Gatti 2002, Basu and Chau 2003).

43. This pattern appears to emerge in data from Bangladesh. For example, Zaman (2000) argued that asset building and empowerment through microcredit were insulating factors notwithstanding the fact that his data showed no consistent pattern of a significantly positive income response to sums borrowed.

The Problem of Interpreting Multiple Indicators

This reasoning seems to imply that a multidimensional set of impacts needs to be tracked, and this is indeed what is done in most studies. Yet, when there are many different impact indicators, there can be a temptation for the overenthusiastic reader to cherry-pick the findings. There is certainly a tendency in the secondary literature for authors to emphasize the positive, even though, taken as a whole, the survey findings are quite mixed or ambiguous. Indeed, one of the most striking features of the primary findings is the remarkably high variance in the measures of impact for specific countries or programs along different dimensions as well as between different programs.

Take, for example, the contrasting findings in the parallel thorough studies carried out by MkNelly and Dunford of Freedom from Hunger (FFH)-backed microfinance programs in Bolivia and Ghana.[44] These careful scholars conducted both baseline and followup surveys, separated by a number of years, and tracked not only clients of the microfinance programs themselves, but two control groups—one drawn from the catchment area of the microfinance program and the other from an uncovered area. Overall, a much more positive program impact was found in Ghana than in Bolivia. Nevertheless, isolated positive results from the Bolivia survey (such as the fact that the incomes of two-thirds of clients had increased after joining the program) have been widely cited in secondary sources, despite the fact that there are relatively few bright spots in the full set of results reported by MkNelly and Dunford. For the program's ultimate objective of improved nutritional status and food security, a large number of indicators were gathered, from which MkNelly and Dunford select fourteen indicators and compare the mean outcomes for participants with two categories of controls. Five of these indicators showed statistically significant differences: four of them unfavorable to the program! Perhaps the control groups chosen in Bolivia just happened to be a very lucky group.[45, 46] In addition to indicators of the ultimate objective, MkNelly and Dunford examined three broad intermediate objectives: women's economic capacity, health and nutrition knowledge, and practice and empowerment.[47] The cited information that the incomes of participants had increased comes from the first of these intermediate objectives, but even here we find a not unambiguous story, for instance, mean nonfarm earnings of participants had *not* increased, while that of nonparticipants

---

44. MkNelly and Dunford (1998, 1999). Examples could be multiplied. Although the Ghana program does well, there is no consistent regional pattern, for example another thorough study by Barnes (2001) for Zimbabwe finds strikingly disappointing impacts (Snodgrass and Sebstad 2002).

45. In the Ghana study the number of significant comparisons (from nine shown) was also five, but this time four of the comparisons were favorable.

46. Sample sizes in such in-depth studies are often rather small for statistical purposes, in this case fewer than 100 households in each of the treatment and the two control groups. Note also that, even though they were not members of the target program, some of the respondents—treatment as well as controls—reported access to other sources of borrowing, a fact which is relevant to the interpretation of such studies as measuring the impact of microfinance in general (as distinct from the impact of a particular microfinance program).

47. Each of the three intermediate objectives is evaluated under a number of subheadings. For women's economic capacity these are: access to credit and loan use, income, nonfarm earnings, personal savings, entrepreneurial skill, food expenditures and household expenditures; for health and nutrition knowledge and practice, the subcategories are breastfeeding, child feeding, diarrhea treatment and prevention, immunization and family planning; and for empowerment the subcategories are: status and decision-making in the household and status and social networks in the community.

had.[48] While the writeup of the original studies fully recognized the sharp contrast between the Bolivia and Ghana findings, the natural tendency to highlight significant (and therefore positive) findings has generated a bias in secondary reportage of these studies, and that pattern is repeated throughout the literature.

Ideally, a meta-analysis of the many impact studies would clarify the position and bring more precision. Unfortunately, the raw materials for a fully satisfactory meta-analysis do not appear to exist. There is no quantitative shortage of indicators reported: change in mean income, or in income from different sources, expressed in dollar terms or as a share of baseline income, or expenditure both total and on selected expenditure categories; change in variability of income or expenditure; increase in savings; change in educational participation, health status and a variety of psycho-sociological indicators. However, the very multiplicity of indicators (and the differing methodologies) means that it is difficult to make comparisons across the various impact studies.

Even if one confines attention to the impact on income, expenditure and wealth, definite conclusions are elusive, especially given many analysts' apparent reluctance to summarize findings in the form of a rate of return, even when it is on the impact of credit that they are mainly focused. With the notable exception of Khandker (1998, 2003), analysts seem to be willing to report almost anything else apart from a rate of return. The point could be quite important: after all, even with a negative rate of return, the borrower's welfare can temporarily be increased by spending borrowed funds on consumption; until the loan is repaid, the simple cash flow will increase the borrower's opportunities. This tendency for analysts to neglect the simplest summary of financial efficiency likely reflects the consideration that the stated goals of most microfinance programs are multidimensional as are the program interventions; they may be reluctant to reduce all to a rate of return on funds borrowed in case that may seem to risk underplaying important dimensions of the program.[49]

Rates of Return on Borrowed Funds Might Be Very High

Without the sense of scale that would be provided by a rate of return (or even better a net present value) calculation, it is hard to make the overall cost-benefit analysis that microfinance now seems to need.[50] Analysts seem satisfied to provide evidence on whether the impact of microfinance access is positive, but without any sense of just how positive. This is odd, especially as the indications are that some survey findings could imply very high annual rates of return on borrowed funds.

For instance, given that we know for Ghanaian borrowers the mean loan size ($60), the mean borrowing period (18 months) and the excess change in income for participants

---

48. A similar result was found in Zimbabwe (Barnes 2001). Here the estimated positive impact of program participation on the consumption of meat and fish by extremely poor households has to be set against a decline in average real income of program participants at a time when mean non-participant real income was increasing.

49. For example the FFH-backed projects, like many other NGO-supported microfinance entities, have an important built-in health and nutrition education program. This makes it difficult to isolate the impact of credit alone, or even of access to microfinancial services in general alone.

50. By comparing the subsidy element with the estimated impact on household consumption, based on the rate of return estimates he had made, Khandker (1998) deduced that cost-benefit ratios were in excess of unity (that is, bad value for money) for lending to male and female borrowers from two of the three credit programs he studied, and for male borrowers in the third. Only Grameen Bank lending to women passed his test.

($17 per month) we can conclude that the financial rate of return was at least 7½ per cent *per month* above the interest rate charged. (That 7½ per cent per month compounds into a jump in income that is at an annual equivalent of 3½ *times* the amount borrowed, an illustration of the power of compounding such high rates of interest.)[51] As indicated, this calculation is an underestimate of the rate of return implied by the Ghana survey data, not least for the reasons given (neglect in the formula of slow-burning returns, use of borrowed resources for risk reduction and other non-measurable benefits, gradual buildup of amount borrowed, and so forth). In principle, an attempt could be made to build these less-tangible factors into the calculation.

The Acute Problem of Sample Selection

Although aggregating the many findings is thus a problem in itself, it pales into insignificance in comparison with the deeper methodological problem of sample selection bias. Even where surveys point to substantial gains in living standards by those who have secured access to microfinance, it is easy to see how this could be an optical illusion. Those households that get access to credit are not likely to be a random draw from the population. Their very success in accessing credit is an indicator of otherwise unmeasured abilities and advantages which themselves will likely have contributed to their economic performance. On its own this phenomenon biases naive estimates in the direction of overstating the impact of credit.

On the other hand, many microfinance NGOs state that they are targeting poor borrowers and may also choose to establish in villages that are relatively poor.[52] This would be a source of bias in the opposite direction. If it is the poorest villages that are targeted by microfinance NGOs, one might observe a misleading positive correlation between access to credit and poverty.

Only if there is some way of disentangling these sources of sample-selection bias can the true impact of access to credit be reliably estimated. Few studies have made a really satisfactory attempt to correct for this major problem.[53] Econometric theory suggests several

---

51. The proposed underlying calculation assumes that the return on the amount borrowed (excess over interest costs) was fully reinvested every month during the months of program participation (and also that there was no borrowing by nonparticipants), and exaggerating slightly by assuming that the final level of borrowing was achieved already from the time of the first (baseline) survey, we can find the internal rate of return by solving: $\Delta y_T / K_T = \{(1 + r)^{1/12} - 1\}(1 + r)^{T/12}$ for r, where K_T is the level of borrowing attained at the time of the follow-up survey, namely quarter T; Δy_T is the difference between income in month T and that in the base period (net of the same calculation for the control group). In the case of Ghana $\Delta y_T = 12 \times US\$17.33 = US\$208$; $K_T = US\$60$; $T = 18$; giving a solution of $r = 1.43$, i.e. excess return over borrowing costs of 143 per cent per annum, or about 7.7 per cent per month. Of course more refined calculations can be made, allowing for a diminishing rate of return to capital, and a gradual build-up of amount borrowed etc. As such, the calculation can be regarded as illustrative.

52. Though in other cases it might be the more dynamic districts that attract the establishment of MFIs.

53. Thus Coleman (1999): "Most existing impact studies are nonacademic project evaluations that are of a descriptive nature or suffer from the selection bias problem." In a useful survey of microfinance impact studies confined to those that tried "to select control groups whose observed characteristics were comparable except for their participation in microfinance," Littlefield, Morduch, and Hashemi (2003) conclude that while "the general pattern of results sheds valid light on the question of impact," "few studies include fully rigorous controls for selection biases." Armendáriz de Aghion and Morduch (2004) write that the differences between anecdotes and statistical evidence "should not be surprising: the anecdotes are culled to show the potential of microfinance, while the statistical analyses are designed to show typical impacts across the board."

possible methods, but each of them is based on strong assumptions.[54] The most promising methods require identifying characteristics that help predict credit access, but are *uncorrelated* with poverty outcomes.

Occasionally a natural experiment seems to allow such identification, as in the data used by Coleman (1999, 2002) where a village banking program was being rolled out to different districts on an essentially random basis. By identifying, in this snapshot, those households who had just enrolled in the soon-to-be-launched village banks, Coleman was able to estimate the propensity to apply for credit of households that had not yet had the benefit of the credit.[55] Using this information, the study suggested that access to the new village bank as a source of credit had little impact on most of the observed outcomes. In essence, it seems that it was households who had good prospects anyway who were applying for credit. It should be noted that the negative finding in this instance may partly reflect the fact that the survey was conducted in a part of Thailand already well-supplied with alternative sources of credit.

Another example of an identifying characteristic that can help the analyst to avoid sample selection bias is the fact that some NGOs try not to lend to households with more than a certain amount of land. By comparing the performance of land-rich households in Bangladeshi villages with credit programs and those without, Pitt and Khandker (1998) were able to take advantage of this practice to identify village-specific unmeasured characteristics. In this case, the correction for sample selection greatly *increased* the estimated impact of credit availability. In effect, the naive estimate found no significant impact of borrowing difference between outcomes such as household consumption; but when account was taken of the fact that participants excluded from the program by its design were higher income households, credit did appear to have an effect—it brought those admitted to the program up to the level of those who had been excluded by design.[56]

---

54. An interesting application of such a method, using propensity score matching to define the control group, is in Legovini's (2002) unpublished study of Nicaragua. She concluded from the evidence that "cash loans, although effective at strengthening growth prospects for the economy overall, are not good policy instruments for reducing poverty."

55. Curiously, although Coleman's paper is often cited as showing the importance of correcting for sample selection bias, there is almost no difference between the estimates that include his key identifying variable and those that don't. (There is a big difference in his highlighted equation explaining women's wealth as between specifications that include their wealth five years ago and those that don't—but that is not part of the correction for sample selection).

56. The widely cited conclusion of Pitt and Khandker (1998) was that every 100 taka borrowed by women (men) raised (annual) household consumption by 18 (11) taka. Many casual readers may have interpreted this as an 18 per cent excess return on capital invested, but that would be an understatement. In particular the time dimensions are important: the amount borrowed here is a cumulative sum over six years—as distinct from the maximum amount outstanding. This consideration seems to imply that a much higher marginal efficiency of capital than 18 per cent. For example, a loan of 1000 taka in each of six years comes to a cumulative borrowing of 6000 taka—about the sample mean for participant women—but this represents an average outstanding loan balance through the period of perhaps 600 taka. Expressing the change in annual consumption as a percentage of this smaller amount would increase the rate of return by a factor of 10. (Independently, Khandker 1998, p. 73, used a production function approach—not specifically related to credit—to estimate a mean return on capital invested by the surveyed households of 48 per cent per annum.) A followup survey, reported in Khandker (2003) suggested much lower returns—about half of what was found in the earlier period. This may possibly be attributable to the increased penetration of microlending in the surveyed districts—to the point where one household in six actually borrows from multiple lenders. This time the availability of a panel allowed first-differencing to eliminate the complication of village and household fixed effects.

Other Measurement Issues

A further consideration which needs to be borne in mind (and which is easier to deal with) is that, even when there are benefits at the individual or household level, displacement effects could be significant. For example, a microentrepreneur who upgrades his capital equipment through credit (buys a bicycle) may simply displace a competitor who hasn't also upgraded (remains working on foot). In order to adjust for displacement effects, the impact on a wider group including the potentially displaced of increased access for some to financial services can be examined. When this is done, for example in analysis of the impact of the presence or otherwise of microfinance services in a rural district (for example, Khandker 2003), or of the branch density of the commercial banking system,[57] the estimated effects on such outcomes as household consumption, and human capital accumulation (school attendance) tend to be small albeit still positive.

Although the above calculations relate to credit and productivity enhancement, in practice, the financial transactions of poor households are more focused on consumption-smoothing than productivity-enhancing activities. This is evident from the kinds of transaction reported in detailed surveys. Interest-free borrowing from and lending to neighbors, relatives and friends, presumably to meet emergency or short-term needs; consumer credit from local shops; saving in coin or with bank deposits: these represent the bulk of financial transactions for surveyed poor households (Rutherford 2000, Ruthven 2001, Ruthven and Kumar 2002, Morduch and Rutherford 2003). Enhancing the efficiency of such activities may not generate a sizable increase in mean income, but it can help stabilize the consumption of poor and near-poor households, thereby reducing the poverty gap and poverty count.

Critics have stressed the fact that additional access to credit could worsen poverty. Among the possible channels for such an effect are the dangers that borrowed money will be squandered leaving the household indebted and further impoverished, or that intra-household friction may be accentuated if women secure access to credit threatening traditional power structures, or if women in fact are constrained to pass the proceeds of borrowing to their menfolk while retaining the obligation to repay (Rahman 1999, Goetz and Sen Gupta 1996).

A fully satisfactory scientific meta-analysis of impact studies is thus impossible. Yet, despite all of these uncertainties, a judgment must be made as to whether promoting microfinance is likely to help reducing poverty. A poll of unbiased observers reading the evidence—both the positive reported experience of practitioners as documented in countless reports and the relatively ambivalent or weak econometric evidence—would at present likely return a cautiously optimistic verdict (for comparable conclusions see for example the reviews by Armendáriz de Aghion and Morduch 2004, Meyer 2002, Morduch 1999, Sebstad and Cohen 2000). The lack of conclusive evidence can be attributed to the difficulty of obtaining data sufficiently rich to convincingly eliminate the possibility of potential biases, but likely owes something to the true effect being considerably smaller than some enthusiasts have hoped. Most researchers seem agreed that microfinance programs are not likely by themselves to lift participants out of poverty in any

---

57. Which has been influenced in India by activist banking policy during the 1980s (Binswanger and Khandker 1995, Burgess and Pande 2004).

short time period.[58] The expectations of non-specialists in this regard may need to be lowered.

More Developed Mainstream Financial Systems are Associated with Less Poverty

Microfinance is not the only means through which an effective financial system can help the poor. Indirect effects operate through the improved functioning of the economy as a whole, reducing involuntary unemployment and underemployment, increasing the scale and efficiency of the national capital stock and with it the demand for and productivity of labor.

It is by now well-established that an effective financial system can make a sizable contribution to enhancing average national prosperity. The share of the population below any given poverty line is closely correlated with average national per capita income. It follows that the financial system's contribution to raising mean incomes in these countries transmits into an important reduction in poverty headcount. Given that almost all of the poor people in the world (measured at the conventional $1 and $2 per day thresholds) are in low or middle-income countries, raising mean income would be enough to eliminate poverty at such abject absolute levels. In view of that, financial sector development could be seen as an anti-poverty tool, even if it did not affect the distribution of income within countries.[59]

It is also plausible that financial sector development could have an additional pro-poor effect, in the sense that economic development trajectories associated with deeper and more efficient financial systems could exhibit less poverty at all levels of mean per capita income. This is consistent with the view of finance espoused by Rajan and Zingales (2003), who argue that access to finance can help erode entrenched monopolies for example by enabling the emergence of competitors that can undermine the power of incumbent firms, and by giving poor households and small-scale producers the means to escape the tyranny of exploitative middlemen.[60]

---

58. This might seem over-cautious given some of the more dramatic reported success stories such as that of Panjaitan-Drioadisuryo and Cloud (1999), surveying the experience of 112 households in Lombok, Indonesia, though their statement, based on a one-shot survey, that "the income of 90% of these families increased enough to move them above the poverty line" perhaps allows the interpretation that (as is suggested by the pattern of data in their Figure 1) many of these respondent households may not have been far below that line at the base date if indeed they were poor at all. The income experience of the controls is not reported. This exemplifies the ambiguity that prevents a simple conclusion from the literature.

59. It may be that considerable progress can be made in increasing per capita income even without the advanced information-intensive dimensions of finance being achieved. This claim would be backed by the findings of Rioja and Valev (2004) that, at low levels of economic development, the quantitative contribution of finance to capital formation seems to be more important than at higher levels. However, an alternative presentation of the data, advanced by Aghion, Howitt and Mayer-Foulkes (2004), reverses this finding. By including the initial level of development as an additional explanatory variable they find that the role of finance is to enable poor countries to escape growth divergence. (Aghion et al. interpret this finding in the context of a model in which weaker access to finance means less investment in technology and therefore a lower probability of leaping to the technological frontier).

60. The opposing view is implied by the model of Greenwood and Jovanovic (1990). They argue that getting involved in the financial sector and benefiting from the screening and risk pooling that it offers requires an initial set-up cost (either of participating in the group that establishes financial infrastructure, or eventually paying an access charge to those who have done so). Poor households will not be in a position to incur this cost, and will not find it worthwhile even to set aside savings for this outlay, hence falling even further behind in the distribution of wealth.

One recently uncovered fact provides evidence suggesting that concentrations of wealth may indeed perpetuate poverty. Specifically, as shown in Honohan (2004), the more concentrated is income at the upper levels of society, the higher is the poverty headcount, even conditional on the mean income *of the non-rich*. This finding is confirmed on a larger sample of 89 countries in Appendix C.

The pro-poor role of finance goes further than this. Deeper financial systems are associated with a lower poverty headcount than would be expected given national per capita income and the distribution of that income between rich and non-rich. New econometric evidence on this point is presented in Appendix C. This presents regression results where, conditioning on mean per capita income *of the non-rich* (as well as on the inflation rate which is well known to be a cross-country correlate of financial depth), financial depth is a significant explanatory variable for the poverty headcount, whether measured relative to the $1 or $2 a day threshold.[61] The statistical significance of the correlation here is seen to be somewhat sensitive to functional form, but nonetheless emerges across a range of specifications. It is an important finding, confirming that to emphasize the financial sector as a key part of the the country's development strategy does not entail making compromises with poverty.[62]

Perhaps it is also true (consistent with the theory of Rajan and Zingales) that, for given financial depth, systems that are associated with more liberal economic regimes generate less poverty. However, attempts to capture this through the inclusion of measures of the institutional and political environment fail to produce robustly significant coefficients. Specifically, we employed institutional variables summarizing:

— the degree to which policy is libertarian (the "economic freedom index" developed by the conservative think-tank Heritage Foundation, and their sub-index relating to banking freedom);
— institutional quality (specifically the simple average of the governance variables reported in the papers by Kaufmann and others (1999 and 2003)—henceforth the "KKZ index");
— the openness of financial regulation (as measured by Barth, Caprio, and Levine's, [2004] index of regulatory restrictiveness).

The most consistent variable here is the economic freedom index, which tends to reduce poverty in most of the specifications shown, but lacking statistical significance. Higher values of the KKZ index curiously seem to be associated with higher poverty, but again this is not a statistically significant effect, except when KKZ and economic freedom are included together, suggesting that this the unexpected coefficient sign is capturing an interaction between the two institutional variables.

Importantly, the impact of mainstream financial development on aggregate national poverty levels is more evident than that of microfinance in these statistical results. Adding

---

61. The rationale for such a specification is discussed more fully in Honohan (2004); using an alternative approach, Beck and others (2004) also find a positive association between financial development and poverty-related indicators, though they look at intertemporal changes rather than levels.

62. It has been suggested that financial liberalization *per se* may adversely affect poverty (Birdsall and Szekely 2003). Poorly designed and sequenced financial liberalizations have been associated with financial crisis, which could have contributed to such an association. (cf. Caprio and others, 2001).

the microfinance penetration variable already described in Chapter 2 to the cross-country regressions produces no significant coefficients (as is shown in Appendix C). This does tend to confirm the impression provided by the project-level literature that escape from poverty through participation in microfinance is slow and uncertain. Part of the reason may be that microfinance remains small relative to the overall financial system, and indeed in most countries microfinance is small relative to the size of the poverty gap. Using the wider penetration variable, including credit from "alternative financial institutions" additional to specialized MFIs does provide some significance, though not when included along with financial depth.[63]

Poverty Gap Data Highlights the Need for Deeper Mainstream Finance in Africa

For most countries, the poverty gap[64] is small in relation to the size of mainstream finance in most countries, but for an important subset of poor countries in Africa it is very large. For these countries achieving greater financial depth seems particularly important if the poverty gap is to be closed.

Figure 6 plots data for 68 countries with poverty gaps in excess of 0.5 per cent of GDP (measured against the $1 a day standard). As such it excludes about 28 developing countries for which the available poverty data indicates a very low poverty gap, as well as all of the advanced economies (which are taken to have a negligible poverty gap measured against this very low poverty threshold). The poverty gap ranges as high as 52 per cent for Nicaragua, with a mean of 12 per cent and a median of about 7 per cent. Plotting the poverty gap against financial depth M2 (and bearing in mind that advanced economies, if shown, would all be found along the x-axis at close to or above 100 per cent) we note a downward trend reflecting the negative correlation between monetary depth and poverty. The diagonal line plotted divides countries on the basis of whether their poverty gap is more than half as large as M2. The eighteen countries to the left of the line, all but one of them in Africa,[65] thus have a high ratio of poverty gap to M2.

The conventional advocacy of policies conducive to greater mainstream financial deepening for the poorest countries is reinforced by this fact, namely that for these countries (the eighteen African countries shown and others like them) the poverty gap is more than 50 per cent of M2. Deeper rather than differently-allocated is the only viable way forward, as a reallocation of existing loanable funds in mainstream finance towards projects of greater benefit to the poor could not go very far towards filling the poverty gap.

Once again, pro-poverty policies suggested by this perspective thus either require, or do not threaten, the development of mainstream finance.

---

63. And the wider concept that measures penetration in terms of deposits and loans at alternative financial institutions, including postal savings banks, is not significant either.

64. This is the minimum aggregate amount, expressed as a percentage of GDP, which, if appropriately distributed, would bring all poor people up to the poverty line.

65. They are Burkina Faso, Burundi, Cameroon, Central African Republic, Ethiopia, The Gambia, Ghana, Lesotho, Madagascar, Malawi, Mali, Mauritania, Nicaragua, Niger, Nigeria, Sierra Leone, Uganda, and Zambia.

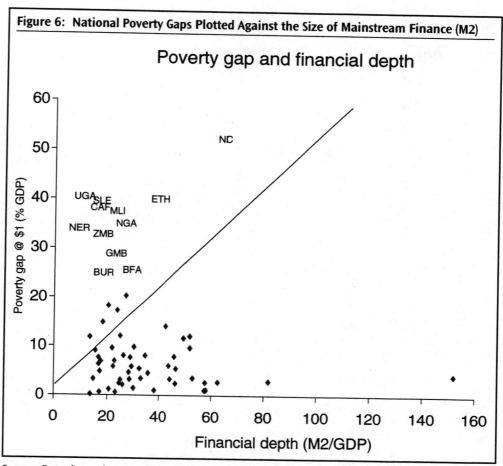

Figure 6: National Poverty Gaps Plotted Against the Size of Mainstream Finance (M2)

Source: Data drawn from World Bank Global Poverty and Inequality Database and IMF: *International Financial Statistics.*

CHAPTER 5

Protecting the Vulnerable

The poor are vulnerable to being badly served by the financial sector. Because this point is often neglected it seems important to provide some discussion of it here even though no new empirical evidence will be offered. The position taken here acknowledges that populist critiques of finance along these dimensions are typically naïve and their proposed policy solutions at best ineffective and more often damaging by impeding welfare-improving contracts and distorting the functioning of finance. Nevertheless, there are, albeit less frequent than is often supposed, instances of abuse that call for policy intervention.

Predatory Lending—The Liberal's Usury

The discussion so far has implied that borrowing at interest is always unproblematic for low income households. That this is not so is sometimes forgotten in the onward rush of microfinance. Poor households can get stuck in a debt trap, as has been stressed by Dale Adams with his provocative insistence on the use of the term "microdebt" in preference to microcredit. An intuitive awareness of the problems underlies the political popularity of usury laws. Indeed interest charges are still misunderstood in many political circles. This is partly because loan-sharking (debt-farming, predatory lending) still exists, and because unaffordable borrowing is employed, inappropriately, as the short-term solution, when disasters and wealth-destroying emergencies occur (Churchill, 2003). (Also, inconsistent and unstable macro policies can result in huge risk premia on wholesale interest rates, and uncompetitive conventional finance combined with unsupportive debt recovery infrastructure result in wide spreads). The solution is not anti-usury laws which, if enforced, can destroy the emergence of microfinance. Instead, a long-term goal would be the adoption of anti-predatory lending laws.[66] Even though this suggestion is likely to be of limited immediate practical value, given lack of effective government institutions, it remains a useful benchmark against which feasible policies can be measured.

Interest Rate Ceilings

If the heart of the campaign to remove financial repression had the modest goal of ensuring that real *ex ante* deposit rates could be positive, it is the microfinance movement that has really placed the long tradition of usury laws under pressure.[67] This movement has clearly established the viability for many borrowers and the necessity for many lenders of high real interest rates for microloans (for a trenchant statement see Robinson 2001). The outlines of the argument are clear: small loans to poor people involve high overheads and direct costs of evaluation and recovery relative to the size of the loan. In addition, there may be relatively high loan-losses for the lender. When these costs, along with the pure rate of interest, are expressed as an annualized percentage, one arrives at a very high break-even rate of interest (especially on short-term loans). Recognition of these points, which tend to be quantitatively more important in the poorest countries, has led to a largely successful campaign to liberalize loan interest ceilings and to allow lenders to enforce the kinds of real rates of interest required to break-even, and these can be in the range 30–40 per cent per annum or even more.

But the political attractiveness of interest rate ceilings remains strong, and seriously constraining ceilings remain in effect in several large countries (including China).

There are some coherent arguments for interest rate ceilings, for example in circumstances where, if banks are recklessly bidding-up lending rates to the point where low-risk projects are being priced-out of the market, an effective ceiling can serve as a selection device between multiple equilibria, without resulting in market disequilibrium (as for example in Hellman et al, 2000). Yet, the conditions under which such models will apply are not frequently observed, and all scholars recognize the adverse effects and side-effects of imposing binding interest ceilings that prevent the profitable extension of credit to high-risk borrowers.

To be sure, the wider issue of unduly high real interest rates in developing countries can be important even when rates are well below what would traditionally be regarded as usurious. Among the causes of high interest rates, those that might be susceptible to pol-

---

66. And the substitution of some feasible combination of insurance (ex ante) and safety-net income support in grant form, rather than emergency loans, in response to poverty-creating catastrophes (Churchill 2003).

67. This would include the absolute prohibition of any return on lending as well as ceilings imposed on rates. Of course the notion of prohibiting a return on capital can no longer command acceptance as it did in medieval times. Even in Islamic jurisprudence, it is now rarely if ever the case that earning a return on financial capital is prohibited outright. Instead, Islamic scholars avoid *riba* by defining contracts that, one way or another, ensure that the return to the provider of funds involves a sharing of profit in which the user of funds is also participating—not just extracting a fee from a needy borrower. That preventing a return on capital would seem unjust nowadays reflects the dominance of the market in economic transactions which embeds an opportunity cost of loanable funds as a base-line for intertemporal transactions. To deprive a lender of the possibility of realizing the time-value of money would represent an expropriation—and an arbitrary one at that, depending on the inflation and risk environment.

icy influence include: lack of macroeconomic credibility resulting in what prove *ex post* to be unnecessarily high risk premia against depreciation or inflation; lack of confidence in the court system resulting in high risk premia against loan-losses; and lack of sufficient competition between financial intermediaries. In each of these cases, the appropriate policy action does not require interest rate ceilings. It is true that interest rate ceilings are still on the books in many advanced economies including many U.S. states. However, the applicability of such ceilings is rather limited in practice.

The debate about interest rate ceilings may be almost over in economic and financial circles, but it still requires to be better understood in political terms. Perhaps politicians do not yet recognize and acknowledge the full systemic consequences of constraining interest ceilings, including: (i) the chilling effect on the expansion of the reach of credit into sectors entailing higher costs and higher risks, (ii) the heightened opportunities for corruption in side-payments for access to credit at below-market rates, and (iii) the effect on diverting savings abroad or into informal channels. Additionally, a heavily indebted government budget is often by far the largest beneficiary in the short-run of a regime of interest ceilings. Highly leveraged big business as well as prosperous but indebted rich households are both also disproportionately sensitive to interest rate movements, and may have a disproportionate influence on policy formation. Finally, politicians often do not see the difference between changes in interest rate levels accomplished by the market-clearing techniques of monetary policy and those effected by administrative fiat.

Predatory Lending

In the rush to liberate credit flows, might something have been neglected? The legislated animosity against usury arose independently in many cultures worldwide and seems to have derived in each case from a perception of the way in which the creditor can exploit the needy debtor. Inhibiting exploitation of the needy remains a widely accepted principle of ethical behavior, not to be rejected as hopelessly idealistic.

Terms such as "predatory lending," "loan-shark," "debt farming," and "debt bondage" are familiar from an extensive literature—including but not confined to the fictional and journalistic—documenting abusive behavior by some lenders to the poor and the misery and social disintegration which can result. This underlying reality would sit uneasily with a wholly laissez-faire attitude to lending at high interest.

To some extent, the observation of a household struggling to repay a debt incurred in bad times may be no more than a manifestation of the household's poverty. Absent other sources of relief, a debt contract freely entered into may be welfare improving for the household even if its servicing pushes the household's consumption close to subsistence and even if it entails debt bondage.[68] However, to stop there would be too Panglossian—because of the unequal distribution of information and power, abuses do occur.

Predatory lending is the term now used in the literature to describe a pattern of abusive behavior in which an unscrupulous lender exploits superior knowledge, especially of financial techniques and legal loopholes, to dupe borrowers into assuming contractual debt obligations

---

68. Debt bondage is defined and outlawed in a 1956 U.N. Convention, but is still being reported (Basu and Chau 2003).

that they cannot hope to meet, likely losing valuable collaterals and transferring over time substantial net economic value to the lender despite defaulting and incurring additional social and psychological penalties.

Thus, predatory lending, as here defined, is not simply a manifestation of poverty, but amounts to the exercise of a fraud.

This is not a problem just for the developing world. Indeed, the rapid expansion in the United States over the past decade or so of what is known as sub-prime lending (lending to individual borrowers at above normal interest rates), including so-called pay-day lending and (in the United Kingdom) "doorstep lending," has been accompanied by growing public concern about abusive behavior on the part of some of the lenders in this market.

The goal of radical policy activists concerned with the over-burdened borrowers has largely shifted away from concern with high interest rates as such. Instead of advocating an absolute ceiling on interest rates, they now seek to eliminate predatory lending, which can thus be seen is the liberal's usury. (See Appendix D for a discussion of why predatory lending cannot be dismissed as unproblematic).

It would be a mistake to assume that developing world money lenders are normally to be classified as predatory lenders. Such studies as Aleem (1990) and Patole and Ruthven (2001) show how moneylenders with great skill and flexibility reach further than the rest of the financial system and cater for marginally creditworthy customers at a low mean *net* return. "They earn a modest profit and do not appear to be socially conservative or exploitative in their lending patterns" (Patole and Ruthven). Yet, it would be naive to deny that predatory lending exists in the developing world, oppressively driving victims deeper into poverty. Indeed, although its extent is impossible to gauge, it is at the center of a number of well-documented abuses of market power (Rutherford 2002).

Policy Against Predation

Finding ways to reduce predatory lending is a worthy goal. Information gaps, imperfect competition and inadequate legal redress for abused borrowers provide the environment in which predatory lending can flourish. These are well-recognized areas for market-strengthening policy in advanced economies. Unlike the market-blocking approach of usury laws, the solution thus builds on developing incentive and information structures whose absence has fed the abuse. A first step is typically "truth in lending" requirements, allowing borrowers to see what they are committing to (such as true interest rates[69]; Christen and others 2003). Credit education and advisory assistance for victims of predation are needed. Requiring lenders to avoid reckless lending can also help. (See Appendix D for further details.)

Unfortunately, the effectiveness of corrective policies along these elaborate lines is questionable in many poor countries. For one thing, the legal and judicial infrastructure is rarely sufficiently advanced to deal adequately with such issues. Furthermore, in countries where protection of creditor rights is not as mechanically assured, predatory lending abuses are less likely to come from formal sector lenders. In poor countries, much of the problem of predatory lending is likely to be found more in an underground or informal economy than in any areas within the scope of formal financial sector policy. For these reasons, predatory

---

69. Even though some fear that making true interest rates apparent could stoke populist demands for ceilings.

lending is a problem for which the solutions of advanced economies, though unlikely to cause harm to the functioning of the financial system, seems of only moderate relevance to combating poverty. Nevertheless, credit education and legal protection for victims should be put in place even if they will not be fully effective at first.

As well as making a start at relieving victims of predatory lending, having a coherent policy against predatory lending can help clarify the essential legitimacy of enforcing creditor rights when predation has not occurred. As such, anti-predator policy could indirectly strengthen the functioning of mainstream finance by reducing the anti-creditor bias often observed in courts and among politicians.

Combating Prejudice and Discrimination

A review of financial sector policy issues affecting the poor would not be complete without some mention of the problems of prejudice and discrimination. The most unattractive feature of a financial system that is closed and "clubby" (to use the term of Rajan and Zingales [2003]) is its *de facto* exclusion of large segments of the community. If the excluded segments are partly defined by ethnicity, geography or other arbitrary dividing lines (such as caste, religion, and so forth), as is all too often the case, then the perpetuation of poverty among the excluded groups is exacerbated.

Discrimination in Practice

Tough legislation against lending discrimination is in place in the United States, yet there is a persistent stream of evidence—albeit not uncontested—which suggests that there may be discrimination against minorities in the mortgage market (Black and others 1978, Blanchflower 2003, Calomiris and others 1994, Ladd 1998, Lindley and others 1994, Munnell and others 1992, Ross and Yinger 2003, Tootell 1996).[70]

Is this differential access due to prejudice or antipathy on the part of lenders, to objective borrower-specific considerations such as lower creditworthiness, or to objective relationship-specific considerations such as the cost of credit appraisal across an ethnic divide? The appropriate policy response will be different in each case.

Information Costs as a Source of Discrimination

Calomiris and others (1994) argue that the two key elements of the U.S. factual evidence: on the one hand, differential procedures being applied to minority borrowers, and on the

---

70. In such a contentious area as this, it is not surprising that these assertions have not gone unquestioned. The review of the debate by Ross and Yinger (2003), while extensive, must be read with some caution (Longhofer 2003). Nevertheless, the evidence does seem to point to the persistence of discrimination of process. As an example, in order to comply with the provisions of the Community Reinvestment Act of 1977, mortgage lenders are constrained to make an adequate amount of lending, but according to Ross and Tootell (2004), lenders may disproportionately require borrowers in unattractive neighborhoods to seek mortgage insurance, thereby reducing their own risk-exposure and increasing the cost of the mortgage. Mortgage applications are more likely to be denied when the housing unit is in a low-income neighborhood if the applicant does not apply for insurance—though if insurance is obtained the approval rate is as good or better than for other neighborhoods.

other hand, higher default rates by minorities, are consistent with an information-based explanation rather than a prejudice-based interpretation. Thus, if lenders experience higher information costs in lending to minorities they will tend to maximize their profits by making lesser efforts to seek out minority applicants and by conducting less-intensive credit appraisal on any such applicants. Then minority borrowers will get less credit, but may still (because of less-effective credit appraisal) experience higher default rates.

The existence in developing countries of relatively closed circuits of credit, where shared ethnicity with the potential lender enhances the borrower's access to credit are frequently mentioned, but little researched. That they do exist is documented rigorously for several African countries by Fisman (2003). The data he uses, combined with his methodology, allow Fisman to throw light on a key question that arises in regard to discrimination in lending, namely whether the discrimination is targeted against certain groups (the same group targeted by all), or whether it also reflects the effects of shared ethnicity. Fisman finds that both effects are present: even among pairs of firms that trade together, shared ethnicity is associated with much more credit. This is certainly consistent with the interpretation that a perceived inability to assess creditworthiness across the ethnic divide is at work.[71]

If differential information-related credit appraisal costs are at the heart of observed discrimination not only in the United States but in developing countries, then information-related solutions policy solutions should be to the fore. Precisely what those information-related solutions should be is less clear given how little we understand about the determinants of the cost of credit appraisal in different contexts. If there are fixed costs or externalities involved, is there a way of subsidizing these without excessive deadweight? For the U.S. context, Calomiris and others suggest that an economically efficient solution would likely see most minority lending being carried out by specialist lenders (presumably co-ethnic with the target group) rather than adopting the approach of seeking that all lenders (including those lacking informational skills in assessing minority applicants) would lend on an equal basis to all ethnic groups, as in the U.S. Community Reinvestment Act of 1977 (CRA; see below).

Given the difficulty of keeping financial sector subsidies on target in developing countries with weak governance institutions is this a safe way of proceeding? These are questions to which the literature as yet offers only incomplete answers.[72]

---

71. Using data from the 1992–5 World Bank Research Program on Enterprise Development, which surveyed firms in five anglophone African countries, Fisman isolates data on trade credit by ethnic group, and whether it was supplied by someone of the same ethnic group. The key question he addresses is whether it is ethnic links, or ethnic background that matters. Not only might ethnic background might be correlated with wealth and other objective indicators of creditworthiness, but prejudice against a certain ethnic group might be general. By taking account of the ethnic identity of the borrowers' major materials suppliers (and not just their sources of credit), the analysis implicitly covers the ethnic dimension of some credit refusals. Firms that source their materials from suppliers of the same ethnicity are more likely to receive trade credit than those whose major materials suppliers are not co-ethnic. Controlling for several other factors, both relationship specific (length, frequency) and borrower specific (size, gender, and so forth), supplier's credit is used about twice as frequently in co-ethnic trading relationships as in others. Part of this can be seen as a ethnic background effect, as Asian and European firms are more than 50 per cent more likely to receive credit than African firms, regardless of the ethnicity of their supplier. Multiple regression shows that ethnic ties do matter as well as ethnic background, at least for the Asian and European group—there does not appear to be such an effect for ethnic-African borrowers, possibly because African materials suppliers tend to be liquidity constrained.

72. See Burgess and Pande (2004) for the sort of evidence which needs to be multiplied.

Prejudice as a Source of Discrimination

It is often whispered, though rarely asserted in official documents, that differential access to credit is attributable not only to information costs, but to prejudice against or antipathy towards certain groups on the part of a country's main lenders. If such prejudices are shared by the political as well as the financial elite, what likelihood is there that policies will ever be introduced to eliminate the credit market effects of prejudice and discrimination? The optimal policy response is then a moot issue in the absence of fundamental political reform.

Where governments have been willing to correct imbalances caused by prejudice and antipathy, they have often reached for nationalization and the establishment of state-owned development finance institutions as possible solutions. Entry of foreign-owned banks may also introduce service provision that is relatively free of prejudice, if their strategic decision-makers are more independent of local ethnic divisions. However, most of these operate with a business plan and cost structure that is unfavorable to delivering financial services directly to the poor.

Among U.S. anti-discrimination policies, the CRA, calling on banks to lend equally to all communities, is often cited as a program that has had few side effects on the functioning of the financial system. At first the program had few teeth (banks were not assessed on whether they actually lent more to target groups) and it may have had very little impact on the pattern of lending (Dahl and others 2000). However, subsequent introduction of sanctions and more energetic monitoring does appear to have resulted in some impact on lending and perhaps a favorable knock-on effect on economic activity in the targeted geographical areas (Litan and others 2001, Zinman 2002). It is less clear whether, by requiring all banks to contribute directly to equalizing credit access, the CRA is the most efficient way of addressing the underlying sources of differential access by borrowers in particular geographic areas or with certain ethnic characteristics.

Many open questions remain in the area of protecting the vulnerable from abuses and prejudice in provision of financial services in developing countries. Political and informational dimensions will be central to the most effective policy approaches. Education and conduct rules are both essential. Although as yet no fully effective off-the-peg solutions can be offered, it is an agenda that should not be neglected.

CHAPTER 6

Concluding Remarks

P olicies that ensure a well-functioning financial system not only contribute to economic growth, but also help reduce poverty more than some other growth enhancing policies. Emphasis on the financial sector is thus a crucial component of a balanced pro-poor development.

The formal, mainstream component of the financial system could do even better in helping overcome poverty through its direct interaction with the poor, or with those segments of the economy which most affect the poor. As competition in the mainstream intensifies, there will likely be progress along this dimension, as mainstream and microfinance begin to converge.

Yet, attempts to ramp up the direct contribution of mainstream financial sector development to poverty reduction through aggressive interventions such as ceilings or subsidies on interest rates can entail significant risks. If the pro-growth functioning of the financial system is adversely affected by misconceived interventions, such attempts are likely to backfire, resulting in a net adverse impact on the poor.

There can also be fiscal costs of such policies, and if so their poverty impact must be judged against alternative uses of public funds for social purposes including education, public health provision and direct income support. However, the risks lie more in the damage that can be done to the bulk of mainstream finance than in regard to the fiscal costs of support for microfinance.

Protecting the functioning of mainstream finance is not a laissez faire blueprint. Protecting the vulnerable against predation and prejudice is a worthy goal in itself and will also help legitimize policies supportive of the development of the sector at large.

To an extent, the debate on where priority in pro-poor financial sector policy should lie—whether favoring mainstream financial development or promoting institutions that offer the poor direct access to financial services—is analogous to the wider economic development debate as to whether tackling growth or inequality should be the priority. Should the emphasis be on increasing the depth and technical efficiency of the mainstream financial system, or on ensuring that the effects of the system at its existing scale reach the poor? This paper finds this to be a false opposition. Both microfinance and mainstream financial development are needed and should be complementary.

Microfinance Penetration

Data Ambiguities

Although there are countless studies of the development of microfinance in different countries, there is no agreement on a uniform indicator of the level of microfinance development. This is partly due to different researchers being focused on different aspects of microfinance:

— Is the researcher interested mainly in direct access of *poor* households to financial services, or is the focus on access of micro-scale enterprises;
— Is the focus on credit, savings, payments, insurance or wider financial services; is the study limited to financial institutions that are specialized in microfinance; or
— Are we also interested in provision of financial services on the micro scale even by mainstream financial institutions?

Data ambiguities are also partly due to the different organizational forms and other institutional arrangements that differ from country to country. Data is often collected on an institutional basis without regard to the type of customer, in which case inclusion of data on an intermediary supplying financial services both at a micro scale and to mainstream clients can be quite misleading, and the extent to which microfinance comes from such broad-based intermediaries varies a lot from country to country.

There are uncertainties at the upper and lower level.

At the lower end, there are a range of rotating and accumulating informal savings associations, pawnbrokers, and so forth. It is really not clear why these should not be included if unlicensed NGO-organized self-help groups are. Hire-purchase arrangements and trader's credit can also represent an active and commercial form of microcredit, yet this is almost never included in statistics.

Even among formal or semi-formal entities, there is no agreement on what to include. Credit unions are a category the admissibility of whose activities can be questioned at both upper and lower margins of microfinance. They may be outside the lower level because they are not always formally licensed as financial intermediaries (thought they are certainly in the formal economic sector—their employees will tend to be caught in the tax net, etc.) Clearly, credit unions can represent a source of financial services (deposit and loan) for the near poor. However, in many countries credit union membership extends quite far up the income scale (with mortgage loans as large as US$100,000 not unknown even in middle-income countries). Including all of their business will tend to overstate what most people think of as microfinance.

At the upper level, banks that are active with lower income and micro-enterprises are increasingly accepted as microfinance providers. This would also include state-owned agricultural development banks and other development banks. Yet, it is not always easy to decide how much of their business should be included. Typically what is done is to confine attention to those banks which have established identifiably separate microfinance arms and include only that business.

Along a different dimension nonbank public development institutions and loan funds are often not counted as part of the financial sector because they are seen as simply fiscal windows, often associated with specific non-finance related policy targets, even though the sums they advance are repayable and represent a revolving fund.

Then there are issues of targeting. Microfinance may mean small loans (with country-specific and quite widely differing ceilings: $5000 in Russia for example). *The Microbanking Bulletin* distinguishes between institutions with a "low-end," broad and "high-end and small business" target markets. Low-end is defined by an average loan-size ceiling of US$150 or 20 percent of national GNP per capita; high-end has average loan size in excess of 150 percent of GNP per capita. However, is the size of loan all that matters, or does it have to be targeted to a relatively poor person; if so how poor? Does gender matter?

If it is not a question of poverty, is microfinance to be delimited by the scale of the enterprise (microfinance=finance for microenterprise). If so, how is microenterprise to be delimited: by the number of employees (for example: my lawyer employs one legal assistant and a secretary) or by turnover (gasoline stations soon exceed plausible ceilings) or profit (in which year—a huge loss-making institution could qualify in some years), or by capital employed (who is going to accurately assess the value of this)?

Explaining Cross-Country Variation in Microfinance Penetration

Because of the uncertainties mentioned above there is in effect no universally acceptable comparable dataset covering the whole world. The two most comprehensive sources, in terms of number of countries covered, are the 2003 report of the Microcredit Summit (Daley-Harris 2003), and an more inclusive inventory—covering savings accounts as well as borrowing, and including institutions that do not specialize in microcredit—which has just been compiled by CGAP (Christen and others 2004).

The CGAP inventory aims to determine how many "poor and near poor" clients have savings or deposits at a broad range of "alternative financial institutions" including not only the "new breed" of specialized MFIs, but also for example mutuals, state agricultural and development banks. The CGAP database also includes postal savings systems and other savings banks which are not in the Microcredit Summit data because they do not make microloans. As such it sets out to be a maximal data set for whatever could be regarded as alternative in the sense of not being a commercial bank. Upwards of 750 million clients of an economic level "not typically served by commercial banks" are estimated[73] for this broad category—only one in four with loans. Commercial banks also offer such services in many countries, but these are not considered "alternative" and as such are not included in the CGAP inventory.[74] (This data is used in the regressions of Appendix C.)

The Microcredit Summit data focuses on borrowing clients of MFIs, and the data is collected as part of an effort to reach a worldwide goal "of reaching 100 million of the world's poorest families, especially the women of those families, with credit for self-employment and other financial and business services by 2005." Although not all of the smaller MFIs report to the Microcredit Summit, the drive to reach this goal provides a presumption that statistical coverage of the target population is reasonably comprehensive. In addition to specialized MFIs, many credit cooperatives and credit unions are included, as are some state development banks.[75] However, many large development banks are not included in the Microcredit Summit data likely because they are not, and do not consider themselves to be, specialized microfinance entities.[76] The Microcredit Summit's focus on credit also excludes, for example, the very large number of clients with savings accounts at postal savings banks. The Microcredit Summit data thus has a narrower focus than that of CGAP both because it aims to measure borrowing clients and also because its institutional coverage is smaller by design—affecting especially China and India.

The Microcredit Summit report presents data on 234 larger institutions representing a very high fraction of the total reach of the population of 2572 reporting institutions to the Summit. Although accounting for less than 10 per cent of the number of reporting institutions, the 234 institutions for which data is available reach 86.2 per cent of the poorest clients reached by the population. These 234 institutions include 55 countries in Latin America, Africa and Asia. (Only three institutions come from Europe: these are ignored in our analysis).

For the purpose of the regressions reported in this appendix, we have defined, from the Microcredit Summit data, a *microcredit penetration* variable taking for each country the

---

73. About one fifth of this total comes from a very approximate imputation for savings banks based on their total assets and certain assumptions about the distribution of savings balances.

74. The largest entities included in the CGAP inventory are: the Postal Savings Banks of India, China, Korea and Egypt (the first two alone account for 234 million savings accounts—about a third of the grand total); India's Regional Rural Banks (network of almost 200 banks); China's Rural Credit Cooperatives (network of 35,000 state-owned intermediaries); Indonesia's National Family Planning Coordinating Board, Bank Rakyat Indonesia (BRI) and the pawn-brokerage Perum Pegadaian; Agricultural Bank of Turkey and Thailand's Bank for Agriculture and Agricultural Co-operatives (BAAC).

75. The largest entities in the Microcredit Summit database are India's National Bank for Agriculture and Rural Development (NBARD); Bangladesh's Rural Development Board (BRDB), Grameen Bank, Association for Social Advancement (ASA); BRAC and PROSHIKA; Indonesia's National Family Planning Coordinating Board and Bank Rakyat Indonesia (BRI); Thailand's Association of Asian Confederation of Credit Unions and Vietnam's Bank for the Poor.

76. Data for China's Rural Credit Cooperatives (47 million loan accounts) and India's Regional Rural Banks (12 million) are striking absentees from the Microcredit Summit report.

aggregate number of clients (not just "poorest" clients) claimed by these institutions and express the result as a percentage of total population. Of course we cannot say that the intermediaries for which data is available account for 86 per cent of clients in each country—this is just the average for the world—nevertheless, given the skewed distribution of intermediary size in each country, there is reason to suppose that the variation in the share of the market accounted for by the largest institutions may not be very great. (This is the variable *Summit* also used in the regressions of Appendix C).

This microcredit penetration variable is distributed highly unequally (Figure 1) and in what appears to be a largely random manner. For example, as seen in Table A1, regressing the penetration variables on population size, GDP per capita or institutional quality produces a marginally significant relationship, according to which a large population, a high GNP per capita (or low poverty) and poor institutions may be associated with *lower* microcredit penetration. Yet, the goodness of fit is low—an R-squared as low as 0.08 if output is measured in logs, rising only to 0.27 even if the two largest outliers, Indonesia and Bangladesh are excluded.[77] Also note that only if output per head and institutions are both included are they individually significant. (This relationship is estimated with log form of the dependent variable—level form regressions perform even worse).[78]

Substituting the poverty rate ($2 a day) for per capita income reduces the number of available countries quite a bit. Now a slightly higher R-squared is obtained and again we find

Table A1: Explaining MFI Penetration (total population)
Dependent variable: Microcredit Summit clients as % total population, by country (log)

Equation:	1.A Coeff.	t-Stat	1.B Coeff.	t-Stat	1.C Coeff.	t-Stat	1.D Coeff.	t-Stat	1.E Coeff.	t-Stat
Constant	2.54	0.8	4.50	*1.5	3.74	1.3	5.92	*2.1	4.62	1.5
Population (log)	−0.134	0.8	−0.247	1.4	−0.215	1.2	−0.341	*2.0	−0.32	1.8
GNP per capita (PPP—level)	−0.253	**3.2	−0.264	**3.5	−0.232	**3.0	−0.241	**3.4	−0.108	1.8
Institutions (KKZ)	1.34	*2.4	1.579	**2.9	1.268	*2.4	1.514	**3.0		
Countries omitted	None		IDN		BGD		BGD, IDN		BGD, IDN	
R-squared / NOBS	0.192	54	0.250	53	0.202	53	0.279	52	0.145	52
Adjusted R-squared	0.143		0.205		0.153		0.234		0.111	
S.E. of regression	1.64		1.55		1.58		1.47		1.58	
Log likelihood	−101.3		−96.5		−97.4		−91.7		−96.1	

77. Clearly the model as specified is not consistent with the idea, advanced in the text, that some threshold effect exists at or about 1 per cent. Exclusion of the two largest outliers could be seen as a gesture in that direction.

78. Inclusion of mainstream financial depth does not significantly improve the fit.

Equation:	1.A'		1.B'		1.C'		1.D'	
	Coeff.	t-Stat	Coeff.	t-Stat	Coeff.	t-Stat	Coeff.	t-Stat
Constant	6.35	1.6	7.08	1.9	8.84	*2.3	9.78	*2.7
Population (log)	−0.167	0.9	−0.256	1.4	−0.277	1.5	−0.378	*2.1
GNP per capita (PPP—log)	−0.560	1.6	−0.474	1.4	−0.640	1.9	−0.553	1.7
Institutions (KKZ)	0.708	1.3	0.656	1.2	0.966	1.8	0.925	1.8
Countries omitted	None		BGD		IDN		BGD, IDN	
R-squared / NOBS	0.076	54	0.091	53	0.129	53	0.162	52
Adjusted R-squared	0.207		0.036		0.076		0.109	
S.E. of regression	1.76		1.69		1.67		1.58	
Log likelihood	−104.9		−100.8		−100.4		−153.0	

Equation:	1.A"		1.B"		1.C"		1.D"		1.E"	
	Coeff.	t-Stat	Coeff.	t-Stat	Coeff.	t-Stat	Coeff.	t-Stat	Coeff.	t-Stat
Constant	1.987	0.6	3.300	1.0	4.408	*2.3	5.97	2.0	4.15	1.3
Population (log)	−0.213	1.1	−0.286	1.5	−0.361	1.9	−0.449	*2.5	−0.346	1.8
Poverty rate ($2 a day)	1.871	1.9	1.591	1.7	2.176	*2.4	1.890	*2.2	0.919	1.1
Institutions (KKZ)	1.350	2.0	1.316	2.0	1.843	**2.8	1.833	**3.0		
Countries omitted	None		BGD		IDN		BGD, IDN			
R-squared / NOBS	0.126	46	0.137	45	0.218	45	0.257	44	0.093	44
Adjusted R-squared	0.063		0.074		0.161		0.202		0.049	
S.E. of regression	1.71		1.64		1.58		1.48		1.61	
Log likelihood	−87.9		−83.9		−82.44		−77.5		−81.9	

*, ** means significant at the 5% and 1% level respectively. Method: OLS.

Dependent variable: Microcredit Summit clients (% total population) by country (log)						
Equation:	**1.F′**		**1.G′**		**1.H′**	
	Coeff.	**t-Stat**	**Coeff.**	**t-Stat**	**Coeff.**	**t-Stat**
Constant	12.38	*2.6	34.76	**3.4	19.22	*2.6
Population (log)	−0.596	*2.4	−1.517	**3.3	−0.807	*2.4
GNP per capita (PPP—level)	−0.266	**3.0	−0.204	1.4	−0.322	*2.7
Institutions (KKZ)	1.588	1.9	−0.791	0.4	1.078	0.8
Banking spread (WDI—log)	−0.986	2.0	−1.509	1.2		
Bank margins (Bankscope—log)			−3.36	2.0	−2.79	2.1
Countries omitted	BGD, IDN		BGD, IDN		BGD, IDN	
R-squared / NOBS	0.327	37	0.706	15	0.544	18
Adjusted R-squared	0.243		0.542		0.404	
S.E. of regression	1.53		1.49		1.57	
Log likelihood	−65.6		−23.4		−30.7	

Equation:	**1.F″**		**1.G″**		**1.H″**	
	Coeff.	**t-Stat**	**Coeff.**	**t-Stat**	**Coeff.**	**t-Stat**
Constant	12.79	*2.6	28.86	*2.4	25.84	**3.9
Population (log)	−0.722	**2.8	−1.517	*3.3	−1.330	**4.2
Poverty rate ($2 a day)	1.624	1.6	6.30	1.2	6.71	**3.3
Institutions (KKZ)	1.530	1.8	1.303	0.4	2.031	1.7
Banking spread (WDI—log)	−1.018	*2.1	0.245	0.1		
Bank margins (Bankscope—log)			−3.94	*2.5	−3.86	**3.4
Countries omitted	BGD, IDN		BGD, IDN		BGD, IDN	
R-squared / NOBS	0.301	33	0.702	14	0.651	17
Adjusted R-squared	0.201		0.516		0.535	
S.E. of regression	1.54		1.49		1.34	
Log likelihood	−58.4		−21.5		−26.1	

(again after deleting Indonesia) that poverty and good institutions both predict a *higher* penetration. Large population continues to act as a negative factor.

When the quoted banking spread (taken as the net from borrowing and lending rates quoted in IFS) is included, the sign is negative (Regression 1.F′). The size of the estimated interest spread effect is quite large. A one-standard deviation shift in this variable is estimated to approximately double microfinance penetration (though it needs to be borne in mind that median penetration is only 0.3 per cent of population). This interest rate effect is consistent

Table A2: Explaining MFI Penetration (poor population)
Dependent variable: Microcredit Summit clients (% of the poor) by country (log)

Equation:	2.A		2.B		2.C		2.D		2.E		2.E	
Income variable:	log(GNPpc)		log(GNPpc)		log(GNPpc)		log(GNPpc)		GNPpc		poverty $2	
	Coeff.	t-Stat	Coeff.	t-Stat	Coeff.	t-Stat	Coeff.	t-Stat	Coeff.	t-Stat	Coeff.	t-Stat
Constant	3.27	0.7	4.04	1.0	8.84	*2.3	7.61	1.9	9.23	**2.8	9.26	**2.9
Population (log)	−0.309	1.5	−0.398	2.0	−0.277	1.5	−0.540	**2.8	−0.528	**2.8	−0.528	**2.7
Income variable	0.284	0.7	0.366	1.0	−0.640	1.9	0.229	0.7	0.009	0.1	−0.829	0.9
Institutions (KKZ)	1.297	1.7	1.256	1.7	0.966	1.8	1.822	*2.6	2.032	**2.8	1.833	**2.8
Countries omitted	None		BGD		IDN		BGD, IDN		BGD, IDN		BGD, IDN	
R-squared / NOBS	0.151	46	0.194	45	0.129	53	0.298	44	0.290	44	0.304	44
Adjusted R-squared	0.091		0.135		0.076		0.245		0.237		0.252	
S.E. of regression	1.80		1.72		1.67		1.58		1.59		1.57	
Log likelihood	−90.1		−86.2		−100.4		−80.5		−80.8		−80.3	

*, ** means significant at the 5% and 1% level respectively. Method: OLS.

with the idea that high profitability of mainstream intermediation has an adverse effect on the scale and penetration of microfinance. Note however that the number of observations here is much smaller.

Sample size shrinks even more if we add available data on banking system net interest margins as a percentage of total assets (average 1995–99). However, this improved measure of the potential profitability of mainstream intermediation displaces the quoted spread and continues to have a strong negative impact on microfinance penetration.[79]

As an alternative specification, we use the penetration expressed as a percentage of poor population. Total population continues to have a negative impact, and institutional quality a positive impact. Per capita income, or poverty level, is insignificant.

Overall the exercise is consistent with the idea that potential market size and good country institutions helps the microfinance industry grow. There is also the suggestion that high profitability of mainstream intermediation can discourage microfinance enterprise.[80] Yet, a huge amount of cross-country variation is not explained by available variables. We can imagine that these unmeasured variables could include enforced usury laws and other microfinance-specific pre-conditions.

---

79. Net interest margins do not, of course provide for non-interest costs and as such are themselves an imperfect measure of the profitability of intermediation. An alternative is the total profit of banks expressed as a percentage of assets (ROA): this too is evidently an imperfect measure of the marginal profitability of lending. Its inclusion (16 available observations) results in an insignificant coefficient.

80. This contrasts, but is not inconsistent with, the observation of Steel and others (1997) for Africa that lack of adequate infrastructures for formal intermediation results in a flourishing of informal microfinance.

MFI Scale and Profitability

This appendix reports the results of a regression exercise linking profitability measured for over 70 microfinance institutions with their scale of operations. The data is drawn from the Microbanking Bulletin (no. 8: 2003), and includes all institutions for which the relevant data is there provided. Two sets of regressions are shown. One uses as dependent variable the so-called "operational self-sufficiency index," that is, operating income expressed as a percentage of the sum of financial expense plus loan loss provision expense plus operating expense. The other has return on total assets as the dependent variable. Note that neither measure makes adjustment for certain hidden subsidies.

As already flagged in the text, and further discussed below, the estimated equations need not necessarily represent a cost function. In particular, many if not most of these institutions are not fully market-driven, and the degree to which they rely on subsidy may not be uncorrelated with their average loan size, or indeed their scale.[81]

In addition to log of total assets as a key explanatory variable, we used a range of alternative measures of the unit size of loans, to capture the idea that small-scale lending may be inherently less profitable. These were average loan size as a percentage of national per capita income ("relative loan size"); the average size of loan, unnormalized; and the share (by number) of loans smaller than US$300. Regional dummies were also included, though only ECA and AFR dummies proved significant in any specification, and the others were not included in the reported specifications. Three wide outliers were removed from the regressions reported.

---

81. Thanks to Rich Rosenberg for urging on me the importance of this point.

The pattern of results is rather clear on the question of institutional scale. Larger firms, whether measured in terms of total assets or number of clients, are more likely to be profitable. The parameter estimate is significant at the 1 per cent in several specifications. Only when too many other variables are included, creating multicollinearity, is statistical significance lost. The size of the impact is also appreciable. A doubling of scale implies between 6 and 10 percentage point improvement in the self-sufficiency index.

Results using individual loan size variables are less clearcut but, as expected, average loan size and the share of small loans having positive and negative impacts respectively on profitability and sustainability when they enter significantly. These findings suggests plausibly that small loans are less profitable.

It would be less easy to rationalize the negative sign on the *relative* loan size variable (which is not very strongly correlated with average loan size (R=0.49). However, it turns out that the significance of this coefficient is entirely due to one observation for which the relative loan size is by far the largest in the sample (at 350 per cent, twice the next largest), and also had a very low self-sufficiency rate of 14 per cent. The third panel shows the implications of excluding this high-leverage observation: the relative loan size is not significant (while the impact of scale is unchanged). (Specifications not repeated in the third panel are essentially unaffected by this exclusion.)

The statistical association observed here are open to multiple interpretations. Many of the institutions involved are not profit-maximizing. There may be a negative correlation between the size of losses made (subsidies received) and the *target* loan size of the institution, for example if a disproportionate number of the more heavily subsidized MFIs target poor clients. These matters warrant more detailed examination.

Table B1: Sustainability, Size, and Focus
(Scale variable: Total assets)

Equation: Variable	1.1 Coeff.	t-Statistic	1.2 Coeff.	t-Statistic	1.3 Coeff.	t-Statistic	1.4 Coeff.	t-Statistic	1.5 Coeff.	t-Statistic	1.6 Coeff.	t-Statistic	1.7 Coeff.	t-Statistic	1.8 Coeff.	t-Statistic
Constant	-0.977	*2.5	-0.918	*2.0	-0.977	1.9	-0.897	1.8	0.286	0.5	0.103	0.2	-0.856	1.8	0.061	0.1
log (Total assets)	0.135	**5.2	0.138	**4.5	0.136	**3.7	0.135	**3.8	0.084	2.0	0.086	*2.1	0.133	**4.3	0.088	*2.1
Relative loan size[a]			-0.216	**2.8							-0.268	**2.8	-0.216	**2.8	-0.283	**2.8
Average loan size ($000)					0.124	0.5	-0.050	0.2	-0.426	1.1						
Small loans (%<$300)									-0.471	2.0	-0.285	1.4			-0.298	1.4
Region: Africa							-0.202	*1.9	-0.237	1.8			-0.096	0.9	-0.066	0.5
Region: ECA							0.194	1.5	0.311	1.9			0.214	1.8	0.218	1.3
MFIs omitted	5, 18, 28		5, 18, 28		5, 18, 28		5, 18, 28		5, 18, 28		5, 18, 28		5, 18, 28		5, 18, 28	
R-squared / NOBS	0.291	69	0.283	60	0.268	55	0.371	55	0.380	33	0.251	39	0.351	60	0.311	35
Adjusted R-squared	0.280		0.258		0.240		0.321		0.265		0.179		0.304		0.193	
S.E. of regression	0.361		0.356		0.359		0.339		0.319		0.355		0.345		0.352	
Log likelihood/ Method	-26.5	OLS	-21.7	OLS	-20.1	OLS	-16.0	OLS	-5.7	OLS	-11.3	OLS	-18.7	OLS	-9.8	OLS

(Scale variable: Clients)

Equation:	1.9		1.10		1.11		1.12		1.13		1.14		1.15		1.16	
Variable	Coeff.	t-Statistic	Coeff.	t-Statistic	Coeff.	t-Statistic	Coeff.	t-Statistic	Coeff.	t-Statistic	Coeff.	t-Statistic	Coeff.	t-Statistic	Coeff.	t-Statistic
Constant	-0.193	0.7	-0.053	0.1	-0.333	0.8	-0.395	1.0	0.482	1.1	0.513	1.3	-0.307	0.8	-0.265	0.7
log (Clients)	0.133	**4.4	0.110	**2.9	0.131	**3.3	0.144	**3.7	0.108	*2.6	0.100	*2.4	0.146	**3.9	0.128	*3.1
Relative loan size[a]			-0.066	0.8							-0.209	*2.2	-0.052	0.7	-0.220	*2.4
Average loan size ($000)					0.639	**2.8	0.454	*2.1	-0.152	0.4						
Small loans (%<$300)									-0.531	*2.4	-0.444	*2.1			-0.487	*2.5
Region: Africa							-0.203	1.9	-0.237	1.9			-0.182	1.6	-0.109	0.8
Region: ECA							0.263	1.9	-0.375	*2.4			0.335	*2.6	0.318	1.9
MFIs omitted	5, 18, 28		5, 18, 28		5, 18, 28		5, 18, 28		5, 18, 28		5, 18, 28		5, 18, 28		5, 18, 28	
R-squared / NOBS	0.236	64	0.152	59	0.235	54	0.368	54	0.431	33	0.281	35	0.323	59	0.405	35
Adjusted R-squared	0.223		0.121		0.205		0.317		0.325		0.212		0.272		0.302	
S.E. of regression	0.385		0.391		0.370		0.34		0.305		0.348		0.356		0.327	
Log likelihood/ Method	-28.7	OLS	-26.7	OLS	-21.4	OLS	-16.3	OLS	-4.3	OLS	-10.6	OLS	-20.1	OLS	-7.3	OLS

(Exclusion of additional outlier)

Equation:	1.2'		1.6'		1.7'		1.8'		1.9'		1.14'		1.15'		1.16'	
Variable	Coeff.	t-Statistic	Coeff.	t-Statistic	Coeff.	t-Statistic	Coeff.	t-Statistic	Coeff.	t-Statistic	Coeff.	t-Statistic	Coeff.	t-Statistic	Coeff.	t-Statistic
Constant	-0.823	1.8	0.295	0.4	-0.614	1.3	0.472	0.7	-0.155	0.3	0.620	1.5	-0.153	0.4	-0.433	1.1
log (Assets/Clients)	0.131	**4.1	0.070	1.6	0.114	**3.5	0.055	1.3	0.096	*2.4	0.083	1.8	0.124	**3.3	0.100	*2.4
Relative loan size[a]	-0.156	1.5	-0.165	1.3	-0.086	0.8	-0.081	0.6	0.004	0.0	-0.134	1.1	0.082	0.9	-0.062	0.5
Average loan size ($000)																
Small loans (%<$300)	-0.282	1.3	-0.282	1.3			-0.294	1.5			-0.415	2.0			-0.436	*2.3
Region: Africa					-0.136	1.2	-0.149	1.1					-0.221	*2.0	-0.184	1.3
Region: ECA					0.257	*2.2	0.324	1.9					0.371	**2.9	0.397	*2.5
MFIs omitted	5, 18, 28, 113		5, 18, 28, 113		5, 18, 28, 113		5, 18, 28, 113		5, 18, 28, 113		5, 18, 28, 113		5, 18, 28, 113		5, 18, 28, 113	
R-squared / NOBS	0.228	59	0.148	34	0.333	59	0.304	34	0.094	52	0.168	32	0.324	58	0.389	34
Adjusted R-squared	0.201		0.063		0.284		0.179		0.061		0.085		0.273		0.280	
S.E. of regression	0.357		0.353		0.338		0.330		0.390		0.348		0.343		0.309	
Log likelihood/ Method	-21.4	OLS	-10.7	OLS	-17.1	OLS	-7.3	OLS	-26.2	OLS	-10.3	OLS	-17.7	OLS	-5.0	OLS

Notes: Dependent variable: Operational self-sufficiency index: operating income as percentage of (financial expense + loan loss provision expense + operating expense).
These cross-sectoral regressions include all MFIs for which the data for 2001 were publicly available, with the exception (as noted) of three small MFIs: SEAP of Nigeria (5), HPPPFI of the Philippines (18) and CCODER of Nepal (28), which were wide outliers in the regressions; the third section of the table also excludes Mikrofond of Bulgaria (113).
[a] Average outstanding loan size as % of GNP per capita.
*, ** denote significance at 5% or 1% respectively. Method: OLS.

Table B2: Return on Assets, Size, and Focus

Equation:	2.1		2.2		2.3		2.4		2.5		2.6		2.7		2.8	
Variable	Coeff.	t-Statistic	Coeff.	t-Statistic	Coeff.	t-Statistic	Coeff.	t-Statistic	Coeff.	t-Statistic	Coeff.	t-Statistic	Coeff.	t-Statistic	Coeff.	t-Statistic
Constant	-1.272	**4.9	-0.842	**3.6	-0.815	**3.0	-0.802	**2.9	0.080	0.2	-0.197	0.5	-0.812	**3.3	-0.157	0.4
log (Total assets)	0.081	**4.7	0.055	**3.5	0.050	*2.6	0.051	*2.7	0.020	0.9	0.024	1.1	0.053	**3.3	0.022	1.0
Relative loan size[a]			-0.040	0.9							-0.090	1.4	-0.038	0.9	-0.085	1.3
Average loan size ($000)					0.147	1.0	-0.072	0.5	-0.099	0.4						
Small loans (%<$300)									-0.326	2.0	-0.260	*1.7			-0.259	1.8
Region: Africa							-0.085	1.3	-0.176	1.9			-0.063	0.9	-0.116	1.2
Region: ECA							0.076	1.0	0.153	1.4			0.085	1.2	0.106	1.0
MFIs omitted	5, 18, 28		5, 18, 28		5, 18, 28		5, 18, 28		5, 18, 28		5, 18, 28		5, 18, 28		5, 18, 28	
R-squared / NOBS	0.255	67	0.179	59	0.203	54	0.253	54	0.366	31	0.174	33	0.229	59	0.273	33
Adjusted R-squared	0.243		0.150		0.172		0.193		0.239		0.088		0.171		0.138	
S.E. of regression	0.261		0.205		0.209		0.206		0.207		0.222		0.202		0.215	
Log likelihood/ Method	-4.1	OLS	11.4	OLS	9.4	OLS	11.2	OLS	8.2	OLS	5.0	OLS	13.3	OLS	7.1	OLS

| Equation: | 2.9 | | 2.10 | | 2.11 | | 2.12 | | 2.13 | | 2.14 | | 2.15 | | 2.16 | |
Variable	Coeff.	t-Statistic	Coeff.	t-Statistic	Coeff.	t-Statistic	Coeff.	t-Statistic	Coeff.	t-Statistic	Coeff.	t-Statistic	Coeff.	t-Statistic	Coeff.	t-Statistic
Constant	-0.706	**3.8	-0.430	*2.4	-0.542	**2.9	-0.546	**2.7	-0.021	0.1	-0.061	0.3	-0.526	**2.7	-0.124	0.5
log (Clients)	0.069	**3.5	0.041	*2.2	0.044	*2.3	0.144	*2.4	0.024	1.1	0.026	1.2	0.050	**2.7	0.032	1.5
Relative loan size[a]			0.021	0.4							-0.074	1.2	0.029	0.6	-0.067	1.1
Average loan size ($000)					0.353	*2.7	0.279	*2.1	0.037	0.2						
Small loans (%<$300)									-0.335	*2.1	-0.300	*2.1			-0.294	*2.1
Region: Africa							-0.088	1.2	-0.172	1.9			-0.104	1.5	-0.119	1.3
Region: ECA							0.093	1.1	-0.169	1.6			0.124	1.6	0.134	1.3
MFIs omitted	5, 18, 28		5, 18, 28		5, 18, 28		5, 18, 28		5, 18, 28		5, 18, 28		5, 18, 28		5, 18, 28	
R-squared / NOBS	0.168	63	0.083	58	0.185	53	0.247	54	0.378	31	0.182	33	0.193	58	0.307	33
Adjusted R-squared	0.154		0.050		0.153		0.184		0.254		0.098		0.132		0.179	
S.E. of regression	0.284		0.218		0.213		0.210		0.204		0.221		0.209		0.211	
Log likelihood/ Method	9.0	OLS	7.6	OLS	8.2	OLS	10.3	OLS	8.6	OLS	5.1	OLS	11.2	OLS	7.9	OLS

Notes: Dependent variable: Return on assets: net operating income plus taxes as percentage of average total assets.

These cross-sectoral regressions include all MFIs in *The Microbanking Bulletin* database for which the data for 2001 were publicly available, with the exception (as noted) of three small MFIs: SEAP of Nigeria (5), HPPPFI of the Philippines (18) and CCODER of Nepal (28), which were wide outliers in the regressions.

[a] Average outstanding loan size as % of GNP per capita.

*, ** denote significance at 5% or 1% respectively. Method: OLS.

Poverty Rates and Financial Depth

This annex updates previous work showing the cross-country correlation between poverty and financial depth and seeks—but fails to find—any comparable correlation between poverty and microfinance penetration. In order to detect any influence of financial sector development on poverty, data on the largest available cross-section of countries was employed. We looked at the poverty headcount, measured using the internationally comparable "$1 a day" standards (converted at PPPs and brought to 1993 equivalent terms).[82]

It is well-known that mean national per capita income is a strong correlate of headcount poverty; this is confirmed in Regression 1A of Table C1, where the dependent variable is the percentage of the population with income lower than the $1 a day standard. Inclusion of per capita income in any cross-country econometric analysis of poverty, essentially testing for any modifiers of this relationship. A role for distribution effects is often discussed (Besley and Burgess 2003) and a particular specification argued in Honohan (2004) includes the income share of the top decile as well as the mean income of the remaining 90 per cent as the basic specification to which financial variables may be added (Regressions 1B and 1C).

Honohan (2004) already showed that financial development indicators are significant when added to this basic specification.[83] The major financial depth variable employed is domestic credit; the inflation rate needs to be also included in all specifications that include a financial depth variable because of the sensitivity of equilibrium money demand to inflation.

---

82. It is recognized that poverty is multidimensional and that, even considering income poverty, the headcount is only one measure, albeit the most widely cited. Furthermore it must be stressed that this absolute poverty measure is not strongly correlated across countries with such inequality measures as the Gini coefficient.

83. For comparable results along different dimensions, see Beck and others (2004).

Table C1: Poverty and Financial Depth
(Dependent Variable: $1 per Day Poverty Ratio)

Equation:	1.A Coeff.	t-Stat	1.B Coeff.	t-Stat	1.C Coeff.	t-Stat	1.D Coeff.	t-Stat	1.E Coeff.	t-Stat	1.F Coeff.	t-Stat	1.G Coeff.	t-Stat	1.H Coeff.	t-Stat
Constant	173.6	**11.6	170.6	**12.8	137.8	**8.5	146.9	**7.9	174.0	**5.9	154.4	**8.1	169.9	**6.8	149.4	**9.1
GNI per cap (log)	-18.8	**10.4														
GNI per cap lower 90% (log)			-19.2	**11.4	-17.5	**10.4	-16.9	**7.2	-24.2	**5.4	-18.8	**6.8	-23.4	**8.1	-19.7	**10.7
Share of top 10%					0.574	**3.3	0.612	**3.0	1.08	*2.5	0.725	**3.4	0.948	**2.8	0.698	**3.9
Private credit % GDP (log)							-3.40	1.2	-1.30	0.3	-3.45	1.1				
Inflation (log)							-1.15	0.6	1.29	0.4						
Penetration (log)									2.09	1.2	-0.174	0.2	0.989	0.7	-0.745	1.1
(penetration variable is)									Summit		CGAP		Summit		CGAP	
R-squared / NOBS	0.546	91	0.598	89	0.643	89	0.650	71	0.663	37	0.665	66	0.652	45	0.665	82
Adjusted R-squared	0.541		0.593		0.634		0.629		0.609		0.637		0.627		0.652	
S.E. of regression	15.2		14.2		13.5		14.4		16.2		14.4		15.3		13.4	
Log likelihood	-375.7		-361.5		-356.2		-287.4		-152.2		-266.5		-184.6		-327.0	

The general conclusion on this somewhat larger sample than employed in Honohan (2004) is to confirm the earlier findings. In addition to being statistically significant often at the 5 per cent level, the estimated coefficient is economically sizable. Thus the coefficient of 6.45 in regression 2A implies that a doubling of financial depth would on average be associated with a decline of over 10 percentage points in the poverty headcount.

Statistical significance of domestic credit is somewhat dependent on exclusion of wide outliers, as is seen from comparison of 2A and 1D; the only difference between these two being in the deletion of Nicaragua from 2A. The result of deleting the next widest outliers, Uganda, Tanzania, and Yemen—all of which are more than three standard deviations from the regression line—is shown in 2D.[84]

In an attempt to see whether penetration by micro and alternative financial institutions might have a detectable and systematic impact on poverty headcount, we added three alternative penetration variables as defined below. The first of these ("Summit") is an indicator of microcredit penetration available for some 45 of the countries for which headcount and top decile data is also available. (This variable is also used in Appendix A above). Whether included on its own (for example, Regression 1G), or with financial depth (1E), this variable (*Summit*) was never significant in any of the specifications tried, even when outliers were removed (note that there is no *Summit* observation for Yemen).

Furthermore, when included with financial depth, the latter is now insignificant, even with Nicaragua removed (Regression 2B)—though this is likely more because of the reduced number of observations (at most 37 overlapping data points) than because of multicollinearity, in that (as shown below) the pairwise correlation between these two variables is low.

The broader credit penetration variable *CGAP*, covering alternative financial institutions additional to specialized MFIs, is significant when included on its own with the outliers removed (Regression 2H), with a sign implying that greater penetration reduces poverty. However, it becomes quite insignificant when included with financial depth, with the latter remaining significant.

The third penetration variable, *CGAP-deposits* including deposit penetration as well as loans, remains insignificant, even when included only on its own (Regression 3M).

On this evidence, the indications are that mainstream finance is associated with lower poverty, but that microfinance is not evidently so, though a wider concept of credit penetration, including credit from development banks, may possibly be associated with lower poverty.

What other institutional variables, known for their relevance to financial and wider economic development contribute to lower poverty (additional to those already discussed)? The general equally weighted average of the KKZ institutional indicators (Kaufman, Kraay and Zoido-Lobatón 1999; Kaufman, Kraay, and Mastruzzi 2003), and the Heritage Foundation Freedom Index, as well as finance-specific indicators such as the Banking freedom subindex (Heritage Foundation) and the activities restrictions and entry restrictions variables proposed by Barth and others (2004) were all added to the specifications already presented. Yet, as is illustrated in Table C3, no pattern of significance was detected.

---

84. The results are also somewhat sensitive to functional form. If the financial depth variable is included in levels rather than logs, the statistical significance declines, though it remains significant at 10 per cent.

Table C2: Poverty and Financial Depth (alternative samples)

Equation:	2.A Coeff.	2.A t-Stat	2.B Coeff.	2.B t-Stat	2.C Coeff.	2.C t-Stat	2.D Coeff.	2.D t-Stat	2.E Coeff.	2.E t-Stat	2.F Coeff.	2.F t-Stat	2.G Coeff.	2.G t-Stat	2.H Coeff.	2.H t-Stat
Constant	149.7	**8.8	178.1	**6.4	156.0	**8.9	165.5	**10.8	193.6	***9.3	178.2	**12.1	184.1	***9.5	165.1	**12.2
GNI per cap lower 90% (log)	−15.0	**6.8	−21.1	**4.7	−16.4	**6.3	−17.0	***9.1	−24.6	***7.6	−19.9	***9.6	−24.4	**11.2	−21.3	**14.2
Share of top 10%	0.515	*2.7	0.817	1.9	0.608	**3.1	0.429	*2.7	0.826	*2.6	0.536	***3.5	0.723	**2.8	0.568	**4.1
Private credit % GDP (log)	−6.45	*2.4	−5.02	1.1	−6.77	*2.2	−6.06	**2.7	−2.93	0.8	−5.25	*2.2				
Inflation (log)	−3.39	1.8	−1.607	0.5	−2.77	1.4	−2.48	1.6	−0.391	0.2	−1.629	1.1				
Penetration (log)			1.062	0.6	−0.206	0.3			0.915	0.8	−1.023	1.6	0.314	0.3	−1.457	**2.7
(penetration variable is)	Summit		Summit		CGAP				Summit		CGAP		Summit		CGAP	
Countries excluded	NIC		NIC		NIC		NIC, TZA, UGA, YEM		NIC, TZA, UGA		NIC, TZA, UGA, YEM		NIC, TZA, UGA		NIC, TZA, UGA, YEM	
R-squared / NOBS	0.681	70	0.673	36	0.694	65	0.772	67	0.823	34	0.810	62	0.787	42	0.779	78
Adjusted R-squared	0.661		0.619		0.668		0.757		0.791		0.793		0.770		0.770	
S.E. of regression	13.2		15.3		13.2		10.8		10.8		10.1		11.0		10.1	
Log likelihood	−277.2		−145.9		−256.8		−251.8		−126.0		−228.1		−158.2		−288.8	

Table C3: Poverty and Financial Depth (additional variables)

Equation:	3.A Coeff.	3.A t-Stat	3.B Coeff.	3.B t-Stat	3.C Coeff.	3.C t-Stat	3.D Coeff.	3.D t-Stat	3.E Coeff.	3.E t-Stat	3.F Coeff.	3.F t-Stat
Constant	147.6	**10.4	165.1	**10.7	165.0	**10.7	185.7	**7.9	173.6	**7.8	192.9	**9.9
GNI per cap lower 90% (log)	-18.2	**10.9	-16.0	**7.6	-15.8	**7.4	-14.7	**6.0	-14.4	**5.5	-18.0	**8.0
Share of top 10%	0.381	*2.4	0.480	**2.8	0.478	**2.8	0.387	*2.2	0.335	1.8	0.430	*2.6
Private credit % GDP (log)			-4.55	1.8	-4.62	1.8	-7.87	*2.4	-7.31	2.1	-5.44	2.0
Inflation (log)			-2.52	1.5	-2.53	1.5	-3.79	1.7	-3.24	1.3	-2.16	1.3
Economic freedom index	0.492	0.2	-5.05	1.3	-4.21	0.9	-7.07	1.7	-5.54	1.2	-7.43	1.9
Additional variable					-0.950	0.4	-0.634	0.9	-2.47	0.4	8.04	*2.2
(which variable)					Bnkfree		Restrict		Entry		KKZ	
Countries excluded	NIC, TZA, UGA		NIC, TZA, UGA		NIC, TZA, UGA		NIC, TZA, UGA		NIC, TZA, UGA		NIC, TZA, UGA	
R-squared / NOBS	0.716	83	0.762	66	0.763	66	0.764	42	0.778	35	0.781	66
Adjusted R-squared	0.706		0.743		0.739		0.724		0.730		0.758	
S.E. of regression	10.9		10.8		10.9		9.86		10.1		10.4	
Log likelihood	-313.9		-247.4		-247.3		-151.9		-126.6		-244.8	

(continued)

Equation:	3.G Coeff.	t-Stat	3.H Coeff.	t-Stat	3.J Coeff.	t-Stat	3.K Coeff.	t-Stat	3.L Coeff.	t-Stat	3.M Coeff.	t-Stat
Constant	151.9	**8.8	171.1	**8.6	186.0	***9.6	200.3	**6.4	194.9	***5.7	172.8	**11.8
GNI per cap lower 90% (log)	-18.7	**10.5	-17.9	**7.7	-18.6	**8.0	-18.6	**5.4	-19.0	**4.7	-18.4	**10.0
Share of top 10%	0.426	*2.7	0.456	*2.7	0.373	*2.3	0.260	1.4	0.204	1.0	0.491	**3.2
Private credit % GDP (log)			-6.21	*2.6	-6.10	*2.5	-8.72	*2.7	-7.33	*2.1	-6.05	**2.8
Inflation (log)			-2.27	1.4	-1.82	1.1	-2.71	1.2	-2.21	0.9	-1.71	1.2
Institutions (KKZ)	3.15	1.2	5.18	1.4	6.20	1.8	4.56	0.9	5.66	0.9		
Additional variable					-2.23	1.1	-0.578	0.8	-1.04	0.2	-0.542	0.6
(which variable)					Bnkfree		Restrict		Entry		CGAP-deposits	
Countries excluded	NIC, TZA, UGA		NIC, TZA, UGA		NIC, TZA, UGA		NIC, TZA, UGA		NIC, TZA, UGA		NIC, TZA, UGA	
R-squared / NOBS	0.713	86	0.749	68	0.772	66	0.752	42	0.774	35	0.803	64
Adjusted R-squared	0.702		0.729		0.749		0.709		0.726		0.786	
S.E. of regression	11.2		11.3		10.7		10.1		10.2		10.2	
Log likelihood	-327.6		-258.2		-246.1		-153.0		-126.9		-236.4	

Notes: ** and * indicate significance at the 1% and 5% levels, respectively. Method: OLS
Cross section: all available countries, except as noted. Note GNI per cap is measured at PPP.

It will be evident that the potential of these data series has not been exhausted, and that the cross-country econometric linkages between finance and poverty deserve further study.

Data Used

The sample of countries used was all available country data from the World Bank World Bank GPID database and World Development Indicators as of December 2003. For any country for which poverty data is available for multiple dates, the most recent data is used. In practice, the mean date of the surveys employed is in 1997. Financial depth data (domestic credit 32D divided by GDP 99B)[85] was drawn from *International Financial Statistics*, December 2003 for 2001 or the latest year available.

The *financial penetration* variables are constructed from the 2003 report of the Microcredit Summit (Daley-Harris 2003) and from the CGAP compilation (Christen and others 2004); these sources are discussed in Appendix A above.

— The first of these presents data for some 55 countries from credit-based MFIs reporting to the Microcredit Summit. For each country we took the sum of the number of clients claimed by these institutions and expressed the result as a percentage of total population to obtain the variable *Summit*, which can be taken as an indicator of microcredit penetration (this is the penetration variable also used in Appendix A above).

— The second series takes the total number of credit (loan) accounts for the wider set of "alternative financial institutions" included in the CGAP study and expresses this as a percentage of total population to obtain the series *CGAP*. This data series has observations on 119 countries. (As mentioned in Appendix A, this includes a wider range of development banks than the Summit data, and as such may be regarded as referring to a somewhat wider concept than microcredit).

— A third series, *CGAP-deposits*, takes the aggregated data for loan and deposit accounts in the CGAP compilation and expresses it also as a percentage of total population. Recall that this includes deposit accounts at postal savings banks. There is data for 142 countries.

As shown below, the correlation between the three penetration variables is quite high (R>0.7), but they are not significantly correlated with the share of private credit in GDP. (Also interestingly *Summit* is uncorrelated with *CGAP—Summit*).

Correlation between financial variables (common sample):

	CGAP	CGAP-deposits	Summit
CGAP-deposits	0.728		
Summit	0.701	0.400	
Private Credit	0.102	0.204	0.095

---

85. The widely alternative series, excluding central bank credit and including credit from non-monetary banking institutions (IFS 22D+44D), is highly correlated with IFS 32D and gives very similar results.

Predatory Lending

P redatory lending is not always easy to detect or define. Sometimes it is as simple as a borrower being duped into agreeing to terms and conditions for a loan far more onerous than was available to that borrower from alternative sources. The term "loan shark" would be appropriate there.

However, most of the more severe cases seem to be characterized by a *deliberate* effort on the part of the lender to trap the borrower into agreeing loan terms that they cannot afford to service as part of a tie-in package in which the borrower also makes an overpriced purchase. Typical purchases could be a used car, a structural home improvement, narcotics or illegal cross-border transportation. *The lender's goal is not simply to recover sums advanced,* because in reality the amount advanced was much lower than stated in the loan contract (considering that the tie-in purchase was over-priced). Instead, the lender's goal is *to use the contract to capture as much value from the borrower as possible.* This could include the borrower's home, offered as security. It could also involve the attachment of a part of the borrower's wages, or of a farming borrower's produce (in either case the term "debt farming" would be appropriate). In extreme cases, the phenomenon could justify the term "debt bondage." Information asymmetries are at the heart of the transaction. Not only information about alternative sources of finance and their cost, but about the value of the tie-in purchase. Borrowers may also be ignorant of the degree to which they might be protected by law or more by the community more widely (though when the tie-in purchase is illegal, the legal protection may be limited).

Even ignoring cases with illegal tie-in sales, studies of below-prime lending in the United States have revealed a pattern of predatory lending involving not only high interest rates and high non-interest fees ("packing"), but also a pattern of repeated refinancing ("flipping") of loans (each time involving further fees), and of secured lending to individuals without regard to their ability to pay (allowing the lender to profit from foreclosing on the security).[86] The public outcry at such behavior led in the US to the establishment in 2000 of a high level committee[87] to recommend on any needed policy response.

Though each of the practices complained about could be said to represent contracts voluntarily entered into and as such not evidently requiring public intervention, examination of the pattern of complaints revealed a legitimate cause of concern. Borrowers embroiled in such loan contracts typically start out not only with impaired credit—which immediately places them at a disadvantage in negotiating a new loan, but also with a lack of information and understanding of the contracts presented to them, which are often fraudulently misrepresented as offering savings, when they only add to costs.[88] Many borrowers are also vulnerable to the high pressure sales tactics used by predatory lenders.

Information gaps, imperfect competition[89] and inadequate legal redress thus provide the environment in which predatory lending can flourish. These are well-recognized areas for market-strengthening policy. Unlike the market-blocking approach of usury laws, the solution thus builds on developing incentive and information structures whose absence has fed the abuse.

Predatory lending can thus be thought of as the economic liberal's usury. Where the laissez-faire perspective may deny from first principles the existence of a problem, the new view of predatory lending confirms what common sense and countless case studies affirm, namely that abuses do occur. It also points to a reform approach which, though difficult to put in place, is likely to provide lasting and self-reinforcing relief.

In the U.S. environment, the major tools of policy recommended have been in the dimensions of: (i) warnings; (ii) prohibited characteristics; (iii) education; (iv) pro-competition measures.

An obligation on a lender to advise the borrower when the characteristics of a loan places it into a category likely to be associated with predatory lending provides a useful *warning*. In addition, other U.S. laws mandate disclosure of true interest rates calculated in accordance with a standard formula and as such relatively free of deception.

Among the newly *prohibited* characteristics of loans are those which have in practice been most abused by lenders exploiting the borrowers' limited capacity to foresee the full consequences of a long-term financial contract. For example, the HUD-Treasury committee proposed outlawing repayment structures on a mortgage loan that include a "bullet payment" within the first 15 years of the loan. Such bullet structures can lure naïve borrowers into an

---

86. "In a predatory lending situation, the party that initiates the loan often provides misinformation, manipulates the borrower through aggressive sales tactics, and/or takes unfair advantage of the borrower's lack of information about the loan terms and their consequences. The results are loans with onerous terms and conditions that the borrower often cannot repay, leading to foreclosure or bankruptcy."—U.S. HUD-Treasury Committee (2000).

87. Co-chaired by the Secretaries of Housing and Urban Development (Cuomo) and of the Treasury (Summers).

88. A noteworthy feature of some such loans contracts is the heavy penalties imposed in the case of default. Borrowers who sign such contracts not realizing that they are unlikely to find the loan serviceable can quickly find the total sum owed ramping up to the point where the lender has captured all of the borrower's home equity—as indeed was the lenders intention.

89. The HUD-Treasury report's examination of the sub-prime market suggested that limited competition among sub-prime lenders strengthened their market power.

unaffordable loan contract that virtually guarantees foreclosure. Early repayment penalties are also restricted by law in the US.

Also recommended by the HUD-Treasury committee is a prohibition on loan refinancing, except on terms which provide the borrower with a "tangible net benefit."

Publicly-funded borrower *education* programs (about which sub-prime borrowers must be advised by the lender) have also been proposed by the HUD-Treasury committee. Mandating lenders to draw the borrower's attention to the existence of such programs has also been recommended.

Knowing that they were eligible for loans on better terms would strengthen the bargaining power of borrowers relative to that of each lender. That is the motivation behind proposals that a lender should be obliged to reveal the standard credit score of the borrower. While such a subtle disclosure would be ineffective in the case of a very ill-informed borrower, it could be a powerful *pro-competitive device* for those less ill-informed about the meaning of a credit score. Requiring lenders to report credit histories comprehensively to credit reporting agencies also helps reduce their market power.[90]

Other possibilities include placing a responsibility on the lender to investigate the borrower's ability to pay, and to avoid reckless lending.

Such proposals make sense in the U.S. context. Lenders who fail to perform as required may well begin to find the law catching up with them.[91] (For example, many of these loans in the United States are securitized and sold on to large financial institutions who may in turn be liable for abuses made by the loan originators.) However, they are calibrated to U.S. conditions and to the kinds of abuses common in the sub-prime mortgage market there.[92] Can they be adapted for problems of predatory lending in the Third World? [93]

---

90. Some argue that this kind of rule limits the return to credit appraisal in this market, thereby potentially reducing access to credit. Such arguments will inevitably hinge on matters of degree.

91. Here too, public funding for free legal aid (for borrowers seeking redress) becomes an issue.

92. Note that high interest rates are not the main source of problems in the US sub-prime mortgage market. Most sub-prime mortgages are concluded at spreads above US Treasury Bonds in the 300–700 basis point range.

93. South Africa's Microfinance Regulatory Council, established in 1999, provides one interesting example of an administrative approach to control of abusive lending in a developing country environment.

References

Aghion, Philippe, Peter Howitt, and David Mayer-Foulkes. 2004. "The Effect of Financial Development on Convergence: Theory and Evidence." NBER Working Paper 10358.

Aleem, Irfan. 1990. "Imperfect Information, Screening, and the Costs of Informal Lending: A Study of a Rural Credit Market in Pakistan." *World Bank Economic Review* 4(3):329–49.

Anderson, Siwan, Jean-Marie Baland, and Karl Ove Moene. 2003. "Sustainability and Organizational Design in Informal Groups: Some Evidence from Kenyan Roscas." University of Oslo, Department of Economics, Memorandum No. 17.

Anderson, Siwan, and Jean-Marie Baland. 2002. "The Economics Of ROSCAS And Intra-household Resource Allocation." *Quarterly Journal of Economics* 117(3):963–995.

Armendáriz de Aghion, Beatriz, and Jonathan Morduch. 2004. *The Economics of Microfinance.* Cambridge, MA: MIT Press. Forthcoming.

Banerjee, Abhijit, and Andrew Newman. 1993. "Occupational Choice and the Process of Development." *Journal of Political Economy* 101(2):274–98.

Barnes, Carolyn, with Erica Keogh and Nontokozo Nemarundwe. 2001. "Microfinance Program Clients and Impact: An Assessment of Zambuko Trust, Zimbabwe." USAID, Office of Microenterprise Development. Processed.

Barth, James R., Gerard Caprio, Jr., and Ross Levine. 2004. "Bank Regulation and Supervision: What Works Best?" *Journal of Financial Intermediation* 13(2):205–248.

Basu, Arnab K., and Nancy H. Chau. 2003. "Targeting Child Labor in Debt Bondage: Evidence, Theory, and Policy Implications." *World Bank Economic Review* 17:255–281.

Beck, Thorsten, Asli Demirgüç-Kunt, and Ross Levine. 2004. "Finance and Poverty: Cross-Country Evidence." World Bank Policy Research Working Paper 3338.

Beegle, Kathleen, Dehejia, Rajeev H., and Roberta Gatti. 2003. "Child Labor, Income Shocks, and Access to Credit." World Bank Policy Research Working Paper 3075.

Besley, Timothy, and Robin Burgess. 2003. "Halving Global Poverty." *Journal of Economic Perspectives* 17(3):3–22.

Birdsall, Nancy, and Miguel Székely. 2003. "Bootstraps, Not Band-aids: Poverty, Equity and Social Policy." In John Williamson and P. P. Kucsynski, eds., *After the Washington Consensus.* Washington, D.C.: Institute of International Economics.

Black, Harold, Robert L. Schweitzer, and Lewis Mandell. 1978. "Discrimination in Mortgage Lending." *American Economic Review* 68(2):186–191 (Papers and Proceedings).

Blanchflower, David G., Philip B. Levine, and David J. Zimmerman. 2003. "Discrimination in the Small Business Credit Market." *Review of Economics and Statistics* 85(4):930–43.

Brandsma, Judith. 2004. "The Third Microfinance Survey in the Arab World: Preliminary Results." UNDP. Forthcoming.

Brown, Warren, and Craig F. Churchill. 2000. Insurance Provision in Low-Income Communities: Part II: Initial Lessons from Micro-Insurance Experiments for the Poor. Washington, D.C.: Development Alternatives Inc. http://www.microinsurance centre.org/resources/Documents/Micro-Insurance-Part2.pdf

Burgess, Robin, and Rohini Pande. 2004. "Do Rural Banks Matter? Evidence from the Indian Social Banking Experiment." Centre for Economic Policy Research, London, CEPR Discussion Paper 4211.

Calomiris, Charles W., Charles M. Kahn, and Stanley D. Longhofer. 1994. "Housing-Finance Intervention and Private Incentives: Helping Minorities and the Poor." *Journal of Money, Credit and Banking* 26(3 Part 2) (Special Issue on Federal Credit Allocation: Theory, Evidence, and History):634–674.

Caprio, Gerard, Patrick Honohan, and Joseph E. Stiglitz, eds. 2001. *Financial Liberalization: How Far, How Fast?* New York: Cambridge University Press.

Charitonenko, Stephanie, and S. M. Rahman. 2002. *Commercialization of Microfinance: Bangladesh.* Manila: ADB.

Charitonenko, Stephanie, and Dulan de Silva. 2002. *Commercialization of Microfinance: Sri Lanka.* Manila: ADB.

Charitonenko, Stephanie, and Ismah Afwan. 2003. *Commercialization of Microfinance: Indonesia.* Manila: ADB.

Charitonenko, Stephanie. 2003. *Commercialization of Microfinance: Thailand.* Manila: ADB.

Christen, Robert Peck. 2001. "Commercialization and Mission Drift: The Transformation of Microfinance in Latin America." CGAP Occasional Paper 5.

Christen, Robert Peck, Timothy R. Lyman, and Richard Rosenberg. 2003. *Microfinance Consensus Guidelines.* Washington DC: CGAP.

Christen, Robert Peck, Richard Rosenberg, and Veena Jayadeva. 2004. "Financial Institutions with a Double Bottom Line: Implications for Microfinance." Washington, D.C.: CGAP Occasional Paper 8.

Churchill, Craig. 2003. "Emergency Loans: The Other Side of Microcredit." *Finance for the Poor* (ADB) 4(3):1–6. http://www.adb.org/Documents/Periodicals/Microfinance/ finance_200343.pdf

Coleman, Brett E. 1999. "The Impact of Group Lending in Northeast Thailand." *Journal of Development Economics* 60: 105–141.

———. 2002. "Microfinance in Northeast Thailand: Who Benefits and How Much?" Asian Development Bank ERD Working Paper No. 9.

Dahl, Drew, Douglas Evanoff, and Michael F. Spivey. 2000. "Does the Community Reinvestment Act Influence Lending? An Analysis of Changes in Bank Low-income Mortgage Activity." Federal Reserve Bank of Chicago Working Paper. http://www. chicagofed.org/publications/workingpapers/papers/wp2000_06.pdf

Daley-Harris, Sam. 2003. "State of the Microcredit Summit Campaign Report 2003." Processed. http://www.microcreditsummit.org/pubs/reports/socr/2003/SOCR03-E[txt]. pdf

Dehejia, Rajeev H., and Roberta Gatti. 2002. "Child Labor: The Role of Income Variability and Access to Credit in a Cross Section of Countries" World Bank Policy Research Working Paper 2767.

Dunford, Christopher. 2003. "Adding Value to Microfinance and to Public Health Education—At the Same Time." *Finance for the Poor* (ADB) 4(4):1–4. http://www.adb. org/Documents/Periodicals/Microfinance/finance_200344.pdf

Fisman, Raymond J. 2003. "Ethnic Ties and the Provision of Credit: Relationship-Level Evidence from African Firms." *Advances in Economic Analysis and Policy* 3(1):Article 4. http://www.bepress.com/bejeap/advances/vol3/iss1/art4

Forster, Sarah, Seth Greene and Justyna Pytkowska. 2003. *The State Of Microfinance in Central and Eastern Europe and the New Independent States.* Washington, D.C.: CGAP.

Ghatak, Maitreesh, and Timothy W. Guinnane. 1999. "The Economics of Lending with Joint Liability: Theory and Practice." *Journal of Development Economics* 60:195–228.

Goetz, A. M., and R. Sen Gupta. 1996. "Who Takes the Credit? Gender, Power and Control over Loan Use in Rural Credit Programs in Bangladesh." *World Development* 24(1):45–63.

Greenwood, Jeremy, and Boyan Jovanovic. 1990. "Financial Development, Growth and the Distribution of Income." *Journal of Political Economy* 98(5,1):1076–1107.

Hashemi, Syed, with Maya Tudor. 2003. "Linking Microfinance and Safety Net Programs to Include the Poorest: The Case of IGVGD in Bangladesh." CGAP Focus Note 21.

Hellman, Thomas, Kevin Murdock, and Joseph E. Stiglitz. 2000. "Liberalization, Moral Hazard in Banking and Prudential Regulation: Are Capital Requirements Enough?" *American Economic Review* 90(1):147–65.

Hoff, Karla, and Joseph E. Stiglitz. 1998. "Moneylenders and Bankers: Price-increasing Subsidies in a Monopolistically Competitive Market." *Journal of Development Economics* 55:485–518.

Honohan, Patrick. 2004. "Financial Development, Growth and Poverty: How Close Are the Links?" World Bank Policy Research Working Paper 3203. Also in Charles Goodhart, ed., *Financial Development and Economic Growth: Explaining the Links.* London: Palgrave.

Kaufmann, Daniel, Aart Kraay, and Pablo Zoido-Lobatón. 1999. "Aggregating Governance Indicators." World Bank Policy Research Working Paper No. 2195, Washington, D.C.

Kaufmann, Daniel, Aart Kraay, and Massimo Mastruzzi. 2003. "Governance Matters III: Governance Indicators for 1996–2002." World Bank Policy Research Working Paper.

Khandker, Shahidur. 1998. *Fighting Poverty with Microcredit.* New York: Oxford University Press.

———. 2003. "Micro-finance and Poverty: Evidence Using Panel Data from Bangladesh." World Bank Policy Research Working Paper 2945.

Ladd, Helen. 1998. "Evidence on Discrimination in Mortgage Lending." *Journal of Economic Perspectives* 12(2):41–62.

Legovini, Arianna. 2002. "The Distributional Impact of Loans in Nicaragua: Are the Poor Worse Off?" World Bank. Processed.

Levy, Fred. 2002. "Apex Institutions in Microfinance." *CGAP Occasional Paper* 6.

Lindley, James T., Edward B. Selby, Jr., and John D. Jackson. 1984. "Racial Discrimination in the Provision of Financial Services." *American Economic Review* 74(4):735–741.

Litan, Robert E., Nicolas P. Retsinas, Eric S. Belsky, Gary Fauth, Maureen Kennedy, and Paul Leonard. 2001. "The Community Reinvestment Act after Financial Modernization: A Final Report." Washington, D.C.: U.S. Department of the Treasury.

Littlefield, Elizabeth, Jonathan Morduch, and Syed Hashemi. 2003. "Is Microfinance an Effective Strategy to Reach the Millennium Development Goals?" CGAP Focus Note 24.

Longhofer, Stanley D. 2003. "Review of *The Color of Credit*." *Zeitschrift fur Nationalokonomie* 81(2):193–196.

Matin, Imran, David Hulme, and Stuart Rutherford. 2002. "Finance for the Poor: From Microcredit to Microfinancial Services." *Journal of International Development* 14(2):273–294.

Matin, Imran, and David Hulme. 2003. "Programs for the Poorest: Learning from the IGVGD Program in Bangladesh." *World Development* 31(3):647–665.

MkNelly, Barbara, and Christopher Dunford. 1998. "Impact of Credit with Education on Mothers and Their Young Children's Nutrition: Lower Pra Rural Bank Credit with Education Program in Ghana." Freedom from Hunger Research Paper No. 4, Davis, CA.

————. 1999. "Impact of Credit with Education on Mothers and Their Young Children's Nutrition: *CRECER* Credit with Education Program in Bolivia." Freedom from Hunger Research Paper No. 5, Davis, CA.

Meyer, Richard L. 2002. "Track Record of Financial Institutions in Assisting the Poor in Asia." ADB Institute Research Paper 49.

Morduch, Jonathan. 1999. "The Microfinance Promise." *Journal of Economic Literature*, 37(4):1569–1614.

————. 2003. "Microinsurance: The Next Revolution?" New York University. Processed.

Morduch, Jonathan, and Stuart Rutherford. 2003. "Microfinance: Analytical issues for India." Forthcoming in Priya Basu, ed., *India's Financial Sector: Issues, Challenges and Policy Options*. New York: Oxford University Press.

Munnell, A. H., G. M. B. Tootell, L. E. Browne, and J. McEneaney. 1996. "Mortgage lending in Boston: Interpreting the HMDA Data." *American Economic Review* 86:25–53.

Panjaitan-Drioadisuryo, Rositan D. M., and Kathleen Cloud. 1999. "Gender, Self-Employment and Microcredit Programs: An Indonesian Case Study" *Quarterly Review of Economics and Finance* 39(5):769–79.

Patole, Meenal, and Orlanda Ruthven. 2001. "Metro Moneylenders: Microcredit Providers For Delhi's Poor." University of Manchester Institute for Development Policy and Management Working Paper No. 28.

Patten, Richard H., Jay K. Rosendgard, and Don E. Johnston, Jr. 2001. "Microfinance Success Amidst Macroeconomic Failure: The Experience of Bank Rakyat Indonesia during the East Asian Crisis." *World Development* 29(6):1057–1069.

Pitt, Mark M., and Shahidur R. Khandker. 1998. "The Impact of Group-Based Credit Programs on Poor Households in Bangladesh: Does the Gender of Participants Matter?" *Journal of Political Economy* 106:958.

Rahman, Amiunur. 1999. *Women and Micro-Credit in Rural Bangladesh: An Anthropological Study of Grameen Bank Lending.* Boulder, CO: Westview Press.

Rajan, Raghuram G., and Luigi Zingales. 2003. *Saving Capitalism from the Capitalists,* New York: Crown Business.

Rioja, Felix, and Neven Valev. 2004. "Finance and the Sources of Growth at Various Stages of Economic Development." *Economic Inquiry* 42(1):127–140.

Robinson, Marguerite S. 2001. *The Microfinance Revolution.* Washington DC: The World Bank.

Ross, Stephen L., and John Yinger. 2002. *The Color of Credit.* Cambridge MA: MIT Press.

Ross, Stephen L., and Geoffrey M. B. Tootell. 2004. "Redlining, the Community Reinvestment Act, and Private Mortgage Insurance." *Journal of Urban Economics* 55(2):278–297.

Rutherford, Stuart. 2000. *The Poor and their Money.* Delhi: Oxford University Press (Working Paper version: University of Manchester Institute for Development Policy and Management).

———. 2002. "Money Talks: Conversations with Poor Households in Bangladesh about Managing Money." University of Manchester: Institute for Development Policy and Management, Working Paper No. 45.

Ruthven, Orlanda. 2001. "Money Mosaics: Financial Choice And Strategy In A West Delhi Squatter Settlement." University of Manchester Institute for Development Policy and Management Working Paper No. 32.

Ruthven, Orlanda, and Sushil Kumar. 2002. "Fine-Grain Finance: Financial Choice and Strategy Among the Poor in Rural North India." University of Manchester Institute for Development Policy and Management Working Paper No. 57.

Sebstad, Jennefer, and Monique Cohen. 2000. *Microfinance, Risk Management, and Poverty.* Background Paper for *World Development Report 2001.* World Bank. Processed.

Sen, Amartya. 2000. "Social Justice and the Distribution of Income." In Anthony B. Atkinson and Francois Bourguignon, eds., *Handbook of Income Distribution.* Vol. I. Amsterdam: Elsevier.

Snodgrass, Donald, and Jennefer Sebstad. 2002. "Clients in Context: The Impacts of Microfinance in Three Countries–Synthesis Report." Washington, D.C.: AIMS. Processed.

Steel, William F., Ernest Aryeetey, Hemamala Hettige, and Machiko Nissanke. 1997. "Informal Financial Markets Under Liberalization in Four African Countries." *World Development* 25(5):817–830.

Tootell, G. M. B. 1996. "Redlining in Boston: Do Mortgage Lenders Discriminate against Neighborhoods?" *Quarterly Journal of Economics* 111(4):1049–1079.

Zaman, Hassan. 2000. "Assessing the Poverty and Vulnerability Impact of Micro-credit in Bangladesh: A Case-study of BRAC." Washington, D.C.: World Bank. Processed.

Zinman, Jonathan. 2002. "The Efficacy and Efficiency of Credit Market Interventions: Evidence from the Community Reinvestment Act." Harvard University Joint Center for Housing Studies Working Paper No. CRA02-2.